Intelligent Guides

MW00460853

Southern Burgundy, Beaujolais, and Jura

October 2017 edition

Wines of Southern Burgundy, Beaujolais, and Jura

Benjamin Lewin MW

Copyright © 2015, 2017, Benjamin Lewin

Vendange Press

www.vendangepress.com

Preface

This is one of three guides on Burgundy. It is devoted specifically to the Côte Chalonnaise, Mâcon, Beaujolais and Jura-Savoie. (Guide 4 in the series focuses on the Côte d'Or, and Guide 5 describes Chablis.)

The first part of the guide discusses the regions and their wines; the second part has individual profiles of the top producers. The basic idea is that the first part explains the character and range of the wines, and the second part shows how each winemaker interprets that character.

In the first part I address the nature of the wines made today and ask how this has changed, how it's driven by tradition or competition, and how styles may evolve in the future. I show how the wines are related to the terroir and to the types of grape varieties that are grown, and I explain the classification system. For each region, I suggest reference wines that I believe typify the area; in some cases, where there is a split between, for example, modernists and traditionalists, there may be wines from each camp.

There's no single definition for what constitutes a top producer. Leading producers range from those who are so prominent as to represent the common public face of an appellation to those who demonstrate an unexpected potential on a tiny scale. The producers profiled in the guide should represent the best of both tradition and innovation in wine in the region

In the profiles, I have tried to give a sense of each producer's aims for his wines, of the personality and philosophy behind them— to meet the person who makes the wine, as it were, as much as to review the wines themselves. For each producer I suggest reference wines that are a good starting point for understanding his style. Most of the producers welcome visits, although some require appointments: details are in the profiles.

The guide is based on many visits to the region over recent years. I owe an enormous debt to the many producers who cooperated in this venture by engaging in discussion and opening innumerable bottles for tasting. This guide would not have been possible without them.

Benjamin Lewin

How to read the producer profiles

The second part of this guide consists of profiles of individual wine producers. Each profile shows a sample label, a picture of the winery, and details of production, followed by a description of the producer and winemaker. The producer's rating (from one to four stars) is shown to the right of the name.

The profiles are organized geographically, and each group of profiles is preceded by a map showing the locations of starred producers to help plan itineraries.

A full list of the symbols used in the profiles appears at the start of the profile section. This is an example of a profile:

Hospices de Beaune *, **, or ***

Hospices de Beaune

VOLNAY
Premier Cru
Appellation Volnay Contrôlée
Cuvée Blondeau
Mis en bouteille par
Jean-Luc Aegerter
Négociant-Éleveur à 21710 Meuix-Saint-Georges
13 % vol.   Produit de France   750 ml

Hotel Dieu, Beaune, France
address

03 80 24 44 02

Catherine Guillemot

catherine.guillemot@ch-beaune.fr

Corton principal AOP

Beaune 1er, Nicolas Rolin
red reference wine

Corton Charlemagne, Charlotte Dumay
white reference wine

www.hospices-de-beaune.com

details of producer
60 ha; 400,000 bottles
vineyards & production

The Hospices de Beaune was founded in 1443 by Nicolas Rolin, chancellor of Burgundy, as a hospital for the poor. Standing in the heart of Beaune, the original buildings of the Hotel Dieu, now converted into a museum, surround a courtyard where an annual auction of wines was first held in 1859.The wines come from vineyards held as part of the endowment of the Hospices, and are sold in November to negociants who then take possession of the barrels and mature the wines in their own styles. (Today the auction is held in the modern covered marketplace opposite the Hotel Dieu.) There are 45 cuvées (32 red and 13 white); most come from premier or grand crus from the Côte de Beaune or Côte de Nuits, but because holdings are small (depending on past donations of land to the Hospices) many cuvées consist of blends from different crus (and are identified by brand names). The vines are cultivated, and the wine is made, by the Hospices. For some years the vineyards of the Hospices were not tended as carefully as they might have been, and the winemaking was less than perfect, but the appointment of a new régisseur has led to improvements in the present century. The name of the Hospices is only a starting point, because each negociant stamps his own style on the barriques he buys.

Contents

Overview of Southern Burgundy

There is an almost continuous line of villages producing wine all the way from Dijon at the northern tip of the Côte de Nuits to the southern tip of the Beaujolais only just north of Lyon. Styles change and meld into one another more gradually than you might think. Moving from the Côte de Nuits to the Côte de Beaune, emphasis shifts from red to white wine. The Côte Chalonnaise extends more or less from Chagny (just south of Chassagne Montrachet) to Chalon-sur-Saône, and produces both red and white; the style is lighter for the whites and not so generous for the reds. The Mâconnais extends from Chalon-sur-Saône to Mâcon itself, and is almost exclusively Chardonnay. Its best wines come from Pouilly Fuissé in the southernmost part of the area, only a stone's throw from the border with Beaujolais. Over the border, wine is almost exclusively red, and the grape changes to Gamay. The best wines come from the Crus in the northernmost part. From Côte Chalonnaise through Beaujolais, the best wines can offer real interest at much better value than their more famous counterparts in the more northern part of Burgundy.

Côte Chalonnaise

The five villages of the Côte Chalonnaise extend for about twenty miles to the immediate south of the Côte d'Or. Unlike the monoculture of the Côte d'Or, viticulture is interspersed with other sorts of agriculture. The wines follow the style of the Côte de Beaune, but the fruits achieve less concentration. There is less use of new oak, and the wines are tighter. For the most part, Côte Chalonnaise has its own producers, although some appellations have negociants who have come from the Côte d'Or, the two leading examples being Faiveley in Mercurey and Louis Latour in Montagny.

The Bouzeron AOP is a rare source for Aligoté (the other being the more generic Bourgogne Aligoté). Growers have to decide whether to label their wines as Bouzeron (without mentioning the grape variety, which might therefore come as a surprise to the uninitiated) or whether to admit the variety but to use the lower appellation label of AOP Bourgogne Aligoté.

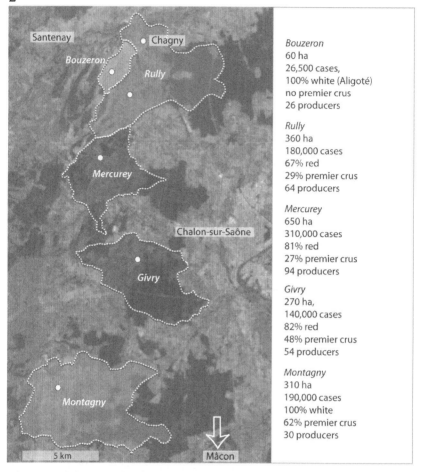

Bouzeron
60 ha
26,500 cases,
100% white (Aligoté)
no premier crus
26 producers

Rully
360 ha
180,000 cases
67% red
29% premier crus
64 producers

Mercurey
650 ha
310,000 cases
81% red
27% premier crus
94 producers

Givry
270 ha,
140,000 cases
82% red
48% premier crus
54 producers

Montagny
310 ha
190,000 cases
100% white
62% premier crus
30 producers

The Côte Chalonnaise has five AOPs.

Aside from Bouzeron, the objective here is to achieve a level of reliability for Pinot Noir or Chardonnay in a mainstream style. With Côte Chalonnaise you don't get the fat, the richness, the uplift of the Côte d'Or, and this is more of a problem for the reds than the whites. The difference from the Côte d'Or is clear if you compare wines directly from those producers who have vineyards in both areas. Both reds and whites are generally best drunk young while still fresh and charming; it's a bit doubtful how much extra complexity is gained by long aging. The limit for whites is usually about five years after release. Reds are best after three or four years, but will last another three or four.

The largest village, Mercurey, makes the firmest red wines, although they sometimes reveal a slightly hard edge. There is a counterpoise between a superficial rich glycerinic sheen to the fruits and that touch of hardness on the finish. Givry produces mostly red wines in much the same style, perhaps not quite as firm. The reds of Rully are lighter. "For me, Rully always has more elegance, finesse; Mercurey has more depth, it's more robust," says Marie Jacqueson in Rully. Similarly, the relatively rare whites of Mercurey or Givry tend to have less overt fruit compared with Rully.

Montagny is an appellation for white wines only. It has the distinction that all its vineyards were classified as premier cru in 1943, although they were reduced when the appellation was extended in 1989. But this still means that premier cru is a less reliable description in Montagny than elsewhere, although only about half the names are used anyway. Montagny also stands out for the loss of independent domains and the rise of the cooperative at Buxy, which now accounts for almost three quarters of production.

Aside from Faiveley, the big name in Mercurey is the Château de Chamirey, where a policy of late picking gives unusually ripe wines for the appellation. Rully is dominated by Vincent Dureuil-Janthial, whose wide range of cuvées from premier crus show unusual refinement for Côte Chalonnaise, and an interesting comparison with his wines from the Côte d'Or. The domain of Paul and Marie Jacqueson is a growing concern that offers an opportunity to compare Rully with Mercurey and Bouzeron. The most

Reference wines for Côte Chalonnaise	
Bouzeron	Domaine A. & P. Villaine Guy Amiot
Givry (red)	François Lumpp, Petit Marole
Mercurey (red)	Paul & Marie Jacqueson, Les Naugues
Mercurey (white)	Château de Chamirey, La Mission
Montagny	Stéphane Aladame, Les Maroques
Rully (red)	Vincent Dureuil-Janthial, Chapitre
Rully (white)	Vincent Dureuil-Janthial, Les Meix Cadot

interesting wines in Montagny come from Stéphane Aladame, who specializes in the premier crus.

The whites are the strongest point of Côte Chalonnaise. At their best they can approach the flavor spectrum of the Côte d'Or, although they rarely achieve the same depth or flavor variety. Reds tend more to show the limitations of the Chalonnaise, but there are definite terroir differences between the appellations.

The Mâconnais

Mâcon stretches from just south of the Côte Chalonnaise to the border with Beaujolais, but very little wine is bottled as Mâcon plain and simple. About 60% of the area is classified as Mâcon Villages, and about 40% of that consists of individual villages whose names can be added after Mâcon, such as Mâcon-Lugny (which accounts for a major part of the individual village wines). Almost all the wine is white, exclusively from Chardonnay, although there is a little red and rosé (from Gamay) in the Mâcon appellation and from some of the individual villages.

Twenty seven villages can attach their names to Mâcon, and most of them are clustered in the southern half of the appellation, where the town of Mâcon itself is situated. Mâcon-Lugny is probably the best known example, and provides a major part of the individual village wines. (The cooperative in Lugny accounts for around a quarter.)

While there are differences in soil types between the villages that potentially affect the character of the wine, they are not as pronounced as in the more famous appellations of, say, the Côte d'Or, and the major importance of the individual village name is to indicate a higher quality level than simple Mâcon Villages. Differences between producers are more important than differences between the villages here.

There are also some individual appellations within the Mâconnais. Viré-Clessé, which was created in 1999 by merging the former village AOCs of Mâcon-Viré and Mâcon-Clessé, is in the center, but the others are located at the southern tip. By far the best known is Pouilly-Fuissé, accompanied by the much smaller satellites of Pouilly-Loché and Pouilly-Vinzelles. Split into two parts, the appel-

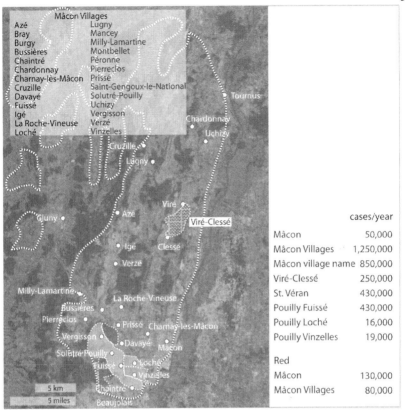

Mâcon Villages	
Azé	Lugny
Bray	Mancey
Burgy	Milly-Lamartine
Bussières	Montbellet
Chaintré	Péronne
Chardonnay	Pierreclos
Charnay-lès-Mâcon	Prissé
Cruzille	Saint-Gengoux-le-National
Davayé	Solutré-Pouilly
Fuissé	Uchizy
Igé	Vergisson
La Roche-Vineuse	Verzé
Loché	Vinzelles

	cases/year
Mâcon	50,000
Mâcon Villages	1,250,000
Mâcon village name	850,000
Viré-Clessé	250,000
St. Véran	430,000
Pouilly Fuissé	430,000
Pouilly Loché	16,000
Pouilly Vinzelles	19,000
Red	
Mâcon	130,000
Mâcon Villages	80,000

The best-known appellations and villages are clustered in the southern part of the Mâconnais.

lation of St. Véran straddles Pouilly-Fuissé and presents wines that used to be labeled as white Beaujolais.

Mâcon is usually a relatively straightforward wine, vinified and matured in stainless steel. The main difference between the named villages and the general Mâcon Villages appellation is a requirement for slightly greater ripeness (a named village must achieve at least 11% natural alcohol, compared with 10.5% for Mâcon Villages), but there is no great change in style, and it would be overly ambitious to try to define differences between individual villages. The main importance of the village name is to indicate higher quality. The general style is for light citrus fruits, without oak influence, with fruit intensity and aromatics depending on the producer and vintage.

The village of Fuissé is in the heart of the Pouilly appellations, surrounded by vineyards on slopes.

There's a feeling that local interests aren't best served by the predominance of negociants who almost all come from the north. Most Mâcon—around three quarters—is made by negociants; four big negociants from Beaune have around 80% of the negociant market. The largest local negociant is Georges Duboeuf, but his focus is mostly on reds from Beaujolais. Yet there has been significant improvement in the quality of Mâcon at all levels in the past couple of decades, partly driven by growers from the Côte d'Or. Comtes Lafon of Meursault came to Milly-Lamartine in 1999, and Domaine Leflaive purchased vineyards in Macon-Verzé in 2003. Undoubtedly the most distinctive local negociant is Maison Verget, established by Jean-Marie Guffens in 1990, following the establishment of Guffens-Heynen as a small grower in 1979.

The wines from Guffens-Heynen mark the full potential of the region, and those of Verget show what can be done within practical limitations. "They are completely different," says Jean-Marie. "When you purchase grapes at Verget, you buy an appellation. When you buy Guffens, you buy a spirit. At Verget I work with pre-printed words but at the domain I have a blank page. We have a philosophy at Verget, but at the domain we don't have a philosophy. At the domain there is no leading idea. At Verget the philosophy is to make good wine within appellation rules at a decent price. We try to make wines as personal as possible, admitting the grapes are not grown as I would grow them. The cost price of picking at the domain is higher than the price I pay for the grapes for Verget."

Part of Jean-Marie's success in redefining the region comes from a difference in perspective. "People say no wood for Macon, but a lot for Bâtard Montrachet because it's a great wine. It's stupid, of course. My view is that all wines have to have the same treatment in order to show the terroir. I change my barrels every five years so there will be no difference between Corton Charlemagne and Mâcon-Vergisson." The Guffens-Heynen wines, from Mâcon-Pierreclos, St. Véran, and Pouilly-Fuissé, all convey a textured impression of coming from grander appellations. With a very wide range of cuvées from Mâcon Villages to Pouilly-Fuissé, Verget's wines offer an unusual opportunity to see what difference terroir makes in the Mâconnais. (Verget also produces many cuvées of Chablis and some of Côte d'Or.) Moving from Mâcon to St. Véran to Pouilly-Fuissé, the Verget wines show increasing fruit concentration and a more subtle range of flavors, rather than changing in style. It's as clear a view of variations in the region as can be found.

Pouilly Fuissé

The great name in the region is Pouilly-Fuissé. "Pouilly-Fuissé used to be a big brand name in the U.S., and visitors were very upset to come here and find only a small village," says Frédéric-Marc Burrier of Château de Beauregard. In fact, there are multiple Pouillys, and in the nineteenth century all the wine was known simply as Pouilly. When the appellation contrôlée was formed, four of the villages decided to join Pouilly-Fuissé, but Loché and Vinzelles stayed out, becoming separate appellations. This may not have been so clever, as Pouilly-Loché and Pouilly-Vinzelles tend to be regarded now as distinctly second rank compared to Pouilly-Fuissé.

The general distinction between the Pouilly's and the surrounding appellations is that the Pouilly vineyards are on the slopes, and at the bottom the AOP changes to Mâcon. So Mâcon-Vinzelles comes from vineyards just below those of Pouilly-Vinzelles. (Simi-

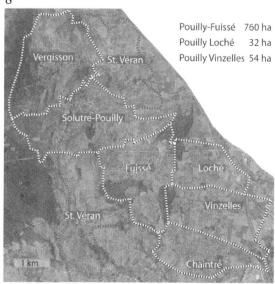

Pouilly-Fuissé   760 ha
Pouilly Loché   32 ha
Pouilly Vinzelles   54 ha

Pouilly-Fuissé consists of four villages; Pouilly Loché and Pouilly Vinzelles are separate appellations. St. Véran consists of two separate areas, one northeast of the Pouillys, the other southwest.

larly, when Viré-Clessé was created from the best parcels on the slopes above the villages in the old Mâcon-Viré and Mâcon-Clessé appellations, the rest became Mâcon Villages.) Pouilly Fuissé is usually aged in oak, and although the tendency to new oak has been reduced (in the old days it often used to cover up the fruits), the style is lighter (and less complex) than the Côte d'Or, but more interesting than Mâcon.

The northern part of the appellation is marked by two calcareous cliff-faces, the Rock of Vergisson and the Rock of Solutré. Vineyards run up to the rocks, but lose the Pouilly Fuissé appellation at high elevations. This may be a consequence of history rather than a reflection of current reality. "The committee of INAO is blind like a horse," says Christine Saumaize-Michelin, whose vineyards are all around the rock of Vergisson. "They won't classify the *climat* above the rock because the elevation is too high, but in the time of global warming, this is completely ridiculous, a north-facing vineyard today is very good."

Pouilly-Fuissé is far from homogeneous. "There is no typicity in Pouilly- Fuissé; it all depends on the villages. Chaintré is always fruity, Vergisson is more mineral," says Jean-Philippe Bret at La Sou-

The famous rock formation of Solutré looms over the vineyards in the northern part of Pouilly-Fuissé.

frandière in Fuissé. The big question then becomes whether to blend across the villages or to represent them in separate cuvées. The trend today is towards defining individual vineyards.

"We are working hard to define premier crus. We think it has been really damaging for Mâcon to be the only area in Burgundy without a hierarchy of appellations," says Frédéric-Marc Burrier, in his capacity as president of the growers association. "We were using our best *climats* with an additional indication on the label before the war in exactly the same way as the Côte d'Or," he says ruefully, "but when Burgundy introduced the premier cru system, here they had a letter asking them to classify premier crus, but the president of the time did nothing about it. So Mâcon became the only part of Burgundy not to have premier crus and we have been paying for that ever since. We studied the history carefully, and we are asking for about 25 different premier crus, which may amount to around 20% of the appellation." The introduction of a hierarchy will also have the effect of encouraging growers to bottle their own wines, which is perhaps a major (unstated) intention.

Terroirs have been much better defined as part of the preparation for premier crus. Frédéric-Marc maintains that, "The reputation of Pouilly-Fuissé for opulent, rich wines is quite wrong, we have wonderful variety of terroirs, we have all those levels mixed up from different geological periods, we have identified fifty different types of soil and geology. There's a million years' difference between the soils. We can find mineral Pouilly-Fuissé and we can find rich Pouilly-Fuissé from clay all over the appellation."

A tasting at Château de Beauregard illustrates the range of terroir differences in Pouilly-Fuissé. Around ten cuvées from different *climats* range from precise and elegant to full bodied. Each is distinctive. And a vertical tasting going back four decades gives a stunning impression of the capacity of Pouilly-Fuissé to age. I would place the wines from seventies in the eighties, and the wines from the eighties in the nineties. These are terrific examples of the potential for aging, achieving a complexity more like what you expect from Meursault than Pouilly-Fuissé.

A move to precision is a common trend at top producers. "What we have at Domaine Ferret is the modern Pouilly-Fuissé, wines that let the grapes speak, and they vary significantly with the terroir. It might be hard to recognize these wines for some who have a stereotypical view of Pouilly-Fuissé with oak covering up the fruits. We are seeing a transparency now that gives a new view of the appellation and the wines," says Audrey Braccini, who took over winemaking at Ferret after Jadot bought the estate.

After tasting through the cuvées of Les Combettes, Le Clos, and Les Brûlées at Château Fuissé, winemaker Antoine Vincent says, "You were asking if there was a single style for Pouilly-Fuissé, here

Reference Wines for Mâconnais	
Mâcon Villages	Maison Verget
Mâcon-Milly Lamartine	Héritiers de Comtes Lafon
Mâcon-Pierreclos	Guffens-Heynen, Le Chavigne
Mâcon-Verzé	Domaine Leflaive
Viré-Clessé	André Bonhomme, Cuvée Spéciale
St. Véran	Guffens-Heynen, Cuvée Unique
Pouilly-Loché	Bret Brothers
Pouilly-Vinzelles	Domaine la Soufrandière, Les Quarts
Pouilly-Fuissé	Château de Beauregard, Les Charmes Château Fuissé, Le Clos Domaine Ferret, Le Clos

you have all three!" The lightest, Les Combettes, comes from deep soils on limestone, and is aged in old barriques. Just behind the winery, the slope of Le Clos has enough variation to justify older oak for the plots at the top and younger oak for the bottom. Les Brulées comes from the most powerful soils of the domain and uses 100% new oak. So here is a completely Burgundian view: "As I go to more powerful soils I use more oak and more new oak."

By the criterion that there is a difference in character and increase in complexity, not merely an increase in reliable ripeness, there are several *climats* in Pouilly-Fuissé that are worthy of individual recognition. The application for premier crus (which must be approved by INAO) has not had universal agreement in the appellation, although most top growers are in support. Its main effect may be not so much to increase recognition (and prices) for the crus, as to counteract the idea of Pouilly-Fuissé as a relatively homogeneous lower-priced alternative to the Côte d'Or, and to place it on its own pedestal.

Beaujolais

Gamay was common all over Burgundy until the twentieth century, but today has almost disappeared from the region, except for Beaujolais, where it is the sole black grape, and accounts for about 95% of plantings. The other 5% is Chardonnay. Beaujolais accounts for about three quarters of the Gamay in France: the rest is found in the Loire or the Rhône, where it is mostly used to make rosé.

Beaujolais is pretty much the only game in town, as there are few alternative possibilities for red wine. There was a fierce dispute between Beaujolais and Burgundy when it appeared that a loophole in the regulations allowed the labels Bourgogne Rouge and Bourgogne Blanc to be used for wine from Beaujolais. "The Burgundy liner is heading straight for the iceberg of Beaujolais, risking drowning those who paid for the voyage," said a statement issued by the Syndicat des Bourgogne.

Responding to this pressure, the rules were changed in 2011 so that only wine from the Beaujolais Crus can be labeled as Bourgogne, but it must say Bourgogne Gamay if it has more than 30% Gamay (which it always does). The appellation Coteaux Bourguignon, which can be made from Chardonnay or Pinot Noir or Gamay from anywhere in the region, can be used by any red Beaujolais.

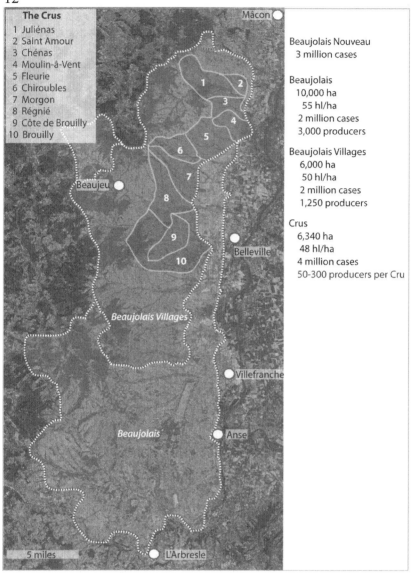

The Crus	
1	Juliénas
2	Saint Amour
3	Chénas
4	Moulin-à-Vent
5	Fleurie
6	Chiroubles
7	Morgon
8	Régnié
9	Côte de Brouilly
10	Brouilly

Beaujolais Nouveau
3 million cases

Beaujolais
10,000 ha
55 hl/ha
2 million cases
3,000 producers

Beaujolais Villages
6,000 ha
50 hl/ha
2 million cases
1,250 producers

Crus
6,340 ha
48 hl/ha
4 million cases
50-300 producers per Cru

Beaujolais AOP largely occupies the southern part of the area. Beaujolais Villages is the northern part, and the crus are located within the Villages region.

Beaujolais falls into three areas. The entire region is entitled to use the description, Beaujolais, but most of the wine labeled as Beaujolais AOP comes from the southern part. The higher level of Beaujolais Villages comes from the northern part. Unlike the Côtes

A view of the hills of the Beaujolais from Croix de Rochefort. Courtesy Beaujolais Vignoble.

du Rhône, where the Villages AOP consists of islands surrounded by the generic appellation, Beaujolais Villages is a large, contiguous area. Within it are the ten crus, each of which is entitled to label its wine solely with the name of the cru.

"Classification in Beaujolais is a matter of granite," says Georges Duboeuf. This is the distinction between the areas of Beaujolais and Beaujolais Villages. A band of granite runs between Mâcon and Villefranche, and more or less fills the width of the Beaujolais Villages. The terrain in the Beaujolais AOP to the south is a mix of sedimentary clay and some limestone.

There is general agreement that Gamay does best on granite. As Gamay is not very widely grown, there isn't much experience in comparing its results on a variety of terroirs. But I suspect that it's not so much that granite is especially suitable for Gamay (rather than other grape varieties), but that it brings a tautness needed to counteract a natural tendency to show blowsy fruits.

Gamay should not be heavy: until the past decade or so, chaptalization was something of a problem in giving the wines an artificial weight. "A lot of people in Beaujolais feel that if you don't have 13% alcohol, your wine won't age; people make a connection between alcohol and quality, but I think that's a big mistake," says Louis-Benoît Desvignes in Morgon. Warmer vintages, and an espe-

Most Beaujolais vineyards are pruned with the free-standing gobelet bush.

cially good run from 2009 to 2012, mean that lately much more of the alcohol has been natural.

Driving through the vineyards, Beaujolais looks different from other regions, because most vineyards follow the old tradition of pruning vines as free-standing bushes. There's a slow move to a more modern trellis system. "The gobelet (local name for the bush) made it easy to protect the vine in winter by heaping earth around, and in cooler summers the soil reflected light up. But honestly, with the winters and summers we have now, we think it's better to have a trellis," says winemaker Cyril Chirouze at Jadot's Château des Jacques. He believes changes will be necessary to respond to global warming. "The most important thing is to change the system of growing, to have more leaves, to be able to adapt to hot conditions. I am more convinced about the need for a change in viticulture than a change in grape varieties. We have to make a lot of changes in the vineyards to make Gamay able to withstand the warmer conditions."

The small amount of white wine that is made in Beaujolais comes from Chardonnay. Some of the villages in Beaujolais can label white wine as Bourgogne Blanc, but otherwise it must be labeled as Beaujolais Blanc. "I think it's very important that Chardonnay continues to be planted in Beaujolais because it is part of our complexity," says Cyril Chirouze. "Beaujolais should not be considered as a homogeneous region. It has a lot of different terroirs, and rosé and white wine as well as red." Château des Jacques produces both Bourgogne Blanc and Beaujolais Blanc, and Cyril draws an interesting distinction between them. "The Bourgogne Blanc has winemaking that's close to Burgundy; half is fermented in barriques. The Beaujolais Blanc is made exclusively in stainless steel."

Production in Beaujolais

Beaujolais has been in crisis for the past half century. Production of Beaujolais has more than halved since 1999, Beaujolais Villages has fallen almost as much, and the crus have fared only a little better. Part of the problem is a perception that Beaujolais means low quality. Indeed, a local magazine, *Lyon Mag*, published an interview with oenologist François Mauss in 2002 under the title "Le Beaujolais, c'est de la merde." The producers did the worst possible thing: they sued for libel. They won a decidedly pyrrhic victory; the resulting publicity did nothing to help Beaujolais. (The award was subsequently overturned on appeal.)

Beaujolais production really falls into four categories: independent producers; cooperatives; negociants; and Georges Duboeuf. Although they are the driving force for innovation, independent producers are the smallest part of the mix. Cooperatives account for more than a third of production. The negociant scene has been changing as the large negociants in Burgundy, just to the north, have seen value in Beaujolais, and have been acquiring the local houses (and sometimes also land). This may lead to an improvement in quality.

For many the region is synonymous with Georges Duboeuf, who established a negociant business in the Beaujolais in 1964. "My ancestors were vignerons at Chaintré for four centuries. I inherited 4 ha of vineyards at Pouilly-Fuissé, not very large, but I was sure of the quality of my wine and started by selling Pouilly-Fuissé everywhere. People said to me, the Pouilly-Fuissé is very good, but we need a good red. So I started to buy and bottle wine," is how Georges recollects the beginning. Known for his remarkable palate and eye for quality, he now produces a range of Beaujolais across all levels. "Hameau Duboeuf," as his winery at Romanèche-Thorins is now signposted, has become a vast enterprise.

By far the largest producer of Beaujolais Nouveau, Duboeuf alone is responsible for a significant part of all Beaujolais production, buying grapes (but no longer wine) from more than 400 growers. Reports variously place Duboeuf's share of all Beaujolais production between 20% and 40%—"Yes, it's something like that," says export manager Romain Teyteau offhandedly when asked for the exact figure. Total production is probably actually around 15-20% of Beaujolais' total of 100 million bottles. While Duboeuf is ineradicably associated with Beaujolais Nouveau, he also produces Beaujolais, Beaujolais Villages, and an extensive series of wines from all the crus, including a substantial number of single vineyard cuvées.

Beaujolais Nouveau

"The most difficult to vinify of all the wines is Beaujolais Nouveau, because it is very fast and depends on technique," Georges says. Beaujolais Nouveau has been at once the resurrection and the downfall of Beaujolais. Beaujolais has always been sold young: called Beaujolais Primeur, through the nineteenth century it was often sold as barrels in which the wine was still fermenting. By the time it reached its destination, it was ready to sell to the consumer! In the twentieth century it was released early in the bistros of nearby Lyon. Today AOP wines cannot be sold until December 15 following the harvest, but an exception is made for "nouveau" wines. The rule now is that Nouveau wine can be shipped from the second Thursday in November in order to be available worldwide for sale a week later.

Beaujolais Nouveau was about 10% of all production when it first became known by this name in the 1950s. Production of Beaujolais doubled by the 1980s, and Nouveau increased to more than a quarter. At the peak it was significantly more than half of all production, but today it's in decline. Sales are falling worldwide, except for Japan, where the rhythm of the annual ritual remains appealing.

In its time, Beaujolais Nouveau was a lifesaver. Sales of Beaujolais were depressed through the 1950s, and the novelty, or perhaps

LES VENDANGES – Un Cuvage en Beaujolais
Départ du vin nouveau

The dispatch of the new vintage of Beaujolais was a sedate affair early in the twentieth century (around 1917).

one might say the gimmick, of Beaujolais Nouveau gave a much-needed lift. Beaujolais Nouveau has always been a marketing phenomenon. Races to get the first Beaujolais Nouveau to Paris or to London by unusual means attracted publicity, at its peak involving a hoopla of balloons, parachutes, racing cars, or even supersonic Concord at the end of the century. The slogan "*Le Beaujolais Nouveau est Arrivé* " became so effective that it was a rare wine shop that did not have it on a placard in the window on November 15.

Nouveau solved a problem by making something that was acceptable to consumers from vineyards that had not been able to succeed with more conventional wine. But the solution lasted only so long as Beaujolais Nouveau was in vogue. The more general problem is not really with Beaujolais Nouveau as such, but with collateral damage. Beaujolais Nouveau is certainly different from other wine; fermentation has barely finished when the wine is bottled, and it might more appropriately be called "fermented grape juice" than wine. But it dominates the image of Beaujolais. Fresh, tart, and (sometimes) fruity, with the aromas of fermentation still much in evidence, it needs to be drunk within a few weeks. Most Beaujolais has always been made for early drinking, but Beaujolais Nouveau is the extreme case.

One of the more successful recent stunts for presenting Beaujolais Nouveau was a motorcycle cavalcade of chefs through New York led by Franck Duboeuf in November 2008. Courtesy Melanie Young.

During the 1970s and 1980s, when the phenomenon peaked, Beaujolais Nouveau really pulled the region out of trouble. But its reputation among more serious wine drinkers is terrible. "The Nouveau has destroyed our image. All of Beaujolais is confused with Nouveau," says Jean-Pierre Large, director of Domaine Cheysson in Chiroubles, pointing to the problem that putting "Beaujolais" on the label is tantamount to telling the consumer that quality (and price) must be limited. "The reputation of Beaujolais is very bad because of Beaujolais Nouveau. But Beaujolais and Beaujolais Villages are made in the same way as the crus," says Baptiste Condemine at Domaine des Souchons. The basic problem is that anything with Beaujolais on the label is stamped with the impression created by Beaujolais Nouveau.

With the exception of some top wines from the crus, Beaujolais is made by a method called semi-carbonic maceration. This requires the vats to be filled with whole clusters of berries (so there is no destemming). Fermentation takes place within the berries, releasing carbon dioxide, which maintains an oxygen-free atmosphere. This is carbonic maceration. However, juice is released from berries that are broken, and the stems form a network allowing the juice to surround the berries. The juice also ferments (conventionally, cata-

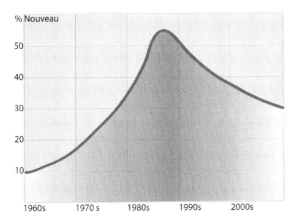

Beaujolais Nouveau rose from a level of 10% in 1960 to a peak of 55% in 1986 before falling to its present 30% of all Beaujolais.

lyzed by yeast), so the overall process is called semi-carbonic maceration.

Typically when the process is about half complete, the free juice is run off, the remaining berries are pressed, the free-run and pressed juice are combined, and fermentation is completed just like for any red wine. The minimal exposure of the juice to the skins means that little tannin is extracted, so that simple fruit flavors dominate the wine, which tends to have a bright purple color. The amount of carbonic maceration is determined by the proportion of whole clusters and the length of time before pressing; it is greatest for Nouveau and least for the crus.

The key feature of Beaujolais Nouveau is its immediate fruitiness. Somewhat controversially, the style has been enhanced by the use of thermovinification. As used in Beaujolais, this involves heating berries to 55 C for 8-12 hours and then cooling them down for fermentation. "This is very current here. It increases color and aromatics. It's mostly used for nouveau and a little bit for Beaujolais and Villages. It's especially useful when the quality of the grapes is not so good," explains oenologist Denis Lapalu at Duboeuf. "It's indispensable in a year such as 2012, it's very much a function of the vintage. Without it we would not be able to achieve the quality in some years," adds Georges Duboeuf.

Thermovinification is controversial because it strengthens the impression of fermentation aromatics. "Unfortunately 90% of Beaujolais today is made by thermovinification—it's terrible," says

Mathieu Lapierre of Domaine Marcel Lapierre in Morgon. The question is really what you want from Beaujolais Nouveau. It's never going to represent terroir.

"In Beaujolais we go from catastrophe to catastrophe. Twenty years ago there were yeasts that made the wine aromatic, hiding the terroir. Today thermovinification is a catastrophe; it's a technique for giving aromas of cassis—but it does it equally for wines from limestone or granite, from Brouilly or Moulin-à-Vent. It does not correspond at all to the idea that the vigneron makes wine to express his vines. It's industrial wine made by technological methods," says Jean-Paul Brun at Domaine des Terres Dorées. Growers who focus on crus agree. "The difference between crus has disappeared at the negociants and producers who are using thermovinification. Thermovinification started in Beaujolais for handling grapes that had problems, for example, damaged by hail, and allowed you to make decent wine; but at the same time it destroyed the best wine. I don't understand how it's possible to do this within the appellation rules, because it destroys the differences between appellations," says Louis-Benoît Desvignes.

Up to half of production from the Beaujolais AOP is Nouveau. Up to a third of Beaujolais Villages is produced as Nouveau, but the crus are not allowed to produce Nouveau. Nouveau is intended for immediate consumption, Beaujolais and Beaujolais Villages should be drunk within a year or so, but some of the crus make wines with ageworthiness.

Beaujolais Crus

"You have to dissociate the crus from Beaujolais. They are apart. There are people who drink only the crus and there are people who drink only Beaujolais Nouveau. The crus are distinguished by terroir and vintage, which is different from Nouveau. One speaks of 2009 as a great vintage, 2010 is different, and so on. Moulin-à-Vent has a reputation more like Burgundy," says Georges Duboeuf.

The crus are allowed to put the name of the cru alone on the bottle (without mentioning Beaujolais), and often do so to minimize the connection with Beaujolais. While this may be helpful for the crus, of course it denies the rest of the Beaujolais any uplift from the halo of its best wines.

The most famous cru of Beaujolais, Moulin-à-Vent, takes its name from the old windmill. Moulin-à-Vent has 663 ha divided into 15 climats, and 280 producers.

The crus offer a wide range of quality, from wine just above Villages standard, to the top wines of Morgon or Moulin-à-Vent, which may be made by conventional vinification and have aging potential. At their best, these can resemble the Côte d'Or. Not every one approves of this. "I do not think they are necessarily any better for it," says Clive Coates MW. "Good Beaujolais... is a light red wine, not at all tannic, purple in color, abundantly fruity and not a bit heavy or sweet." Yet Beaujolais is moving in the direction of weightier wines. "It's very important for us to show that Beaujolais can age," says Anthon Collet of the producers' association Inter Beaujolais.

It's a mistake to regard the best crus as ready for drinking upon release. Those from the top producers need at least another year or so. Perhaps in an exceptional year like 2009 the fruits immediately outweigh the structure, but otherwise there can be enough tannin to obscure the fruits. For the best wines in a good year, the ideal period may be to enjoy them around five years after the vintage; it is only an exceptional wine—perhaps a top Moulin-à-Vent or Morgon—that is likely to last longer than that. At their best, the top crus can be difficult to distinguish from village wines from the Côte de Beaune.

But there is a great range even within the top crus. One of the problems in Beaujolais is that the attempts to make wines with complexity and aging potential from the crus is undercut by wines with prices barely above Beaujolais Villages. As in Burgundy, the producer is the only reliable guide.

Maybe it's time for another revolution, and perhaps the recent study of soil types, represented on the walls of several producers by copies of the multicolored maps showing the soil types in the Crus, has been a contributory factor. Visiting producers, say, twenty years ago, most would have one, or at most two, cuvées from a Cru. Now it is common to find multiple cuvées from each Cru, each representing specific terroirs. The maps are the result of extensive land surveys to support the argument for premier crus, with several candidates in Moulin-à-Vent, Fleurie, and Morgon. In Fleurie the best known *climat* is Grille Midi, a large south-facing amphitheatre that is always warm; in Morgon, it is Côte du Py, a hill that rises to 350m. In Moulin-à-Vent, the best-known *climats* are right under the windmill, with La Roche at the top.

Individual cuvées are a very recent phenomenon, and a move towards a formal hierarchical classification is gathering force. It's a sign of how things are changing that Louis-Benoît Desvignes recollects, "When I started a special bottling (the Vieilles Vignes from Javernières on the Côte du Py) in 2009, people thought I would lose customers." At Château des Jacques, whose vineyards are just below the famous windmill in Moulin-à-Vent, six individual vineyard cuvées have been added to the general blend (which for years was in any case the best wine of the appellation).

There are mixed feelings about the change that premier crus will bring. "In the next five to ten years we will definitely have premier crus. The locomotive is Morgon and Moulin-à-Vent. But it will be both good and bad. People from Burgundy come here to buy land—it's speculation. I'm a peasant, I'm not a financier. The price of land and the wine will increase," Louis-Benoît says. Yet to some extent, an important transition has already taken place with the increasing move toward single vineyard wines by several producers. Recognition of premier crus may simply formalize the premium that already is being paid for the best sites.

Morgon has 1,111 ha and 6 climats. It's best climat, Côte du Py, is a steep hill with a plateau at the top marked by a cross with an inscription that says, "Erected in grateful recognition of the extraordinary harvest of 1906."

"Morgon is the oldest cru of Beaujolais. It was the first because it had the history, it's the best. There's lots of schist. There are six *climats*. Studies of soils and subsoils have been done to define the areas; there will be premier crus in a few years," says Baptiste Condemine at Domaine des Souchons. But he adds, "Many people know Morgon because they know Marcel Lapierre. I think this is more important for us than the premier crus."

Indeed Marcel Lapierre was at the forefront of a revolution led by the "gang of four." The others were Guy Breton, Jean-Paul Thévenet, and Jean Foillard, all friends from the town of Villié-Morgon. Their impetus came from a winemaker called Jules Chauvet, who introduced them to the notion of picking late for full ripeness, selecting to eliminate rotten berries, using natural yeast, minimizing sulfur dioxide, using slow fermentation at low temperature (the proportion of carbonic maceration varies with producer and vintage), and maturing in barriques.

"My father was part of a group that rebelled against the industrial production of Beaujolais," says Mathieu Lapierre, adding, "We try to make natural wines but it's difficult to defend them from the industrial system. We try to master things so as to be as natural as possible, but no one can be superman." It's a measure of his attitude that when asked about global warming, he says, "I'm not sure about that, the real question is why some people in Beaujolais chaptalize; if you reach 12% do you need more alcohol?"

So what is the effect of the new approach on the wines? A single word describes the difference with the average Beaujolais: structure. This is not to imply that the wines are tough, but behind the fruits is the necessary framework to support development. Lapierre's Morgon can in fact be a little hard in the first year or so, but four years after the magnificent 2009 vintage, it showed tense black fruits with earthy overtones, and a real sense of terroir that might be confused, for example, with Pommard. "Morgon should have an aroma of violets and cherries, with flavors of strawberries and a slightly masculine side," says Mathieu. Morgon is serious wine, often giving a taut impression of its granitic terroir, with the greatest purity of line usually to be found in the putative premier cru of Côte du Py.

"The difference between the crus is the terroir. Brouilly is blue stone, Fleurie is pink granite, and Moulin-à-Vent has manganese. The crus are an element in advancing the reputation of the region," says Georges Duboeuf. A tasting with Georges is an education in Beaujolais. Starting with the Beaujolais Villages, the wine is all about fruit. "This is the side of Beaujolais we all like, very juicy and fruity," he says. "You get fruit and freshness and for another year or two you will be able to enjoy it. What we are looking for in Beaujolais Villages is the pleasure of the moment." The distinction between Beaujolais Villages and the lesser crus is the more direct sense of fruit aromatics in the Villages (reflecting more carbonic maceration).

Turning to the crus, in general the lightest, often barely distinguished from better Beaujolais Villages, are Brouilly (the largest), Regnié, and Saint Amour. Côte de Brouilly is distinct from Brouilly (as its name suggests, it lies on the slopes of Mount Brouilly); and with even more elevation, Chiroubles comes from hillside vineyards often over 300m. Tasting with Duboeuf, the flavor spectrum of Brouilly and Chiroubles are generally similar, with more weight than the Villages, but less evident aromatics. Chénas is solid. Then going up the scale of crus, there is more intensity, but not a great change in character. The real difference comes when you reach Morgon, Fleurie, and Moulin-à-Vent. Morgon is taut, Fleurie is soft and fleshy, and Moulin-à-Vent is quite serious and elegant.

Fleurie's symbol is La Madonne, a small chapel on top of a hill that can be seen from all over the appellation. Fleurie has 856 ha and 13 climats. Grille-Midi is the top climat.

Morgon and Moulin-à-Vent have the most distinctive soils, with manganese prominent in both, and iron in the latter. They often seem more Burgundian as they age. Fleurie can be immediately appealing; although vineyards close to Morgon or Moulin-à-Vent sometimes take on the more structured quality of those appellations, in the heart of the appellation, the wines are fleshy. The old description was that Fleurie is the queen of Beaujolais, while Moulin-à-Vent is the king. Morgon has varied terroirs, from the sandier soil of Corcelette, to the more alluvial soil and greater clay of Grand Cras, to the volcanic terroir of Côte du Py.

Moulin-à-Vent always has structure, but if you really want to taste the character that granite gives wine, go to Morgon, especially the Côte du Py, which really shows that taut restraint of granite. It is the most distinctive of the crus. Juliénas, which can be a big, sturdy wine, comes as a surprise, placed in Duboeuf's lineup after the Moulin-à-Vent: while tight and structured, it doesn't have the same tensile impression as Morgon or Moulin-à-Vent. The differences as you ascend the hierarchy are more to do with the balance between fruits and acidity, breadth versus tautness, or intensity of concentration, than the flavor spectrum as such.

Fleurie and Moulin-à-Vent have always been considered ahead of all the other crus, but I would now place Morgon with them. One reason is that young winemakers, who bring new, modern attitudes to the region, such as Julien Sunier or Mee Godard, can more easily buy land in Morgon, where prices are only about two thirds of Fleurie or Moulin-à-Vent. Perhaps this is associated with the increased emphasis on *climats* in Morgon, which is bringing its terroirs into sharper focus.

What is the Real Beaujolais?

The tradition in the region is to mature the wine—even the crus—in cement tanks. Slowly wood has been introduced. Château des Jacques in Moulin-à-Vent—always one of the most ageworthy wines—has done this for decades, and the trend has been accentuated since Jadot acquired the estate in 1996. While initially regarded with some scepticism by others, today there is a definite move in this direction, and many producers in the top crus now have at least one cuvée that is matured in barriques.

Vinification should be a bigger issue than it is: carbonic maceration has become the new tradition, but actually it's a twentieth century phenomenon. "Carbonic maceration started to be used only in the 1950s. Until then, winemaking in Beaujolais was very similar to Burgundy," says Cyril Chirouze at Château des Jacques. "So we consider that the real tradition is to work like Burgundy."

It's clear that carbonic maceration is the lifeblood for Beaujolais Nouveau, and probably necessary for Beaujolais and Beaujolais Villages: but is it appropriate for the crus, or do they make better wines by following Burgundian precepts? The risk with carbonic maceration is that the wine seems superficial, driven by high-toned aromatics in the absence of tannins. This can be lovely in wine for immediate enjoyment, but carbonic maceration is not a technique that brings out terroir differences, so it's somewhat at odds with a move towards defining a hierarchy of premier crus within the top crus.

So what is the real Beaujolais, where is the future of the region? In wines using carbonic maceration to bring out fruits or in wines made more conventionally to balance fruits with structure? Jean-Paul Brun at Domaine des Terres Dorées has had difficulties with his attempts to obtain the AOP agrément for ageworthy wines. He does not use carbonic maceration for any of his wines, not even the Beaujolais. "If you use carbonic maceration it's too short to allow the terroir to express itself. Burgundian vinification for all the wines lasts for 5-6 weeks. A Burgundian vinification has the objective of transmitting the terroir to the wine." If Beaujolais is truly to find a way forward through the classification of premier crus, it's beyond time to stop making difficulties for producers who are making the very wines that should prove the point.

Of course, no one asks the most fundamental question, which is all but unthinkable: is Gamay the best grape to grow in the Beaujolais? Is it time to recognize that it is just a historical accident that Gamay became the grape of Beaujolais, more *faute de mieux* than anything else; would it be a good idea to step back and ask what grape variety would actually make the best wine here?

Reference Wines for Beaujolais	
Beaujolais	Domaine des Terres Dorées, L'Ancien
Beaujolais Villages	Georges Duboeuf
Brouilly	Jean-Claude Lapalu, Vieilles Vignes
Chénas	Paul-Henri Thillardon
Chiroubles	Patrick Bouland
Côte de Brouilly	Domaine des Terres Dorées
Fleurie	Yvon Métras,
Juliénas	Georges Duboeuf, Château des Capitans
Morgon	Marcel Lapierre
Morgon, Côte du Py	Louis & Claude Desvignes Jean Foillard
Moulin-à-Vent	Château des Jacques
Regnié	Charly Thévenet, Grain & Granit
St. Amour	Maison Trénel

The grape that thrives on granite par excellence is Syrah; furthermore, the warming climate has brought Beaujolais close to the temperatures of the Northern Rhône, say, three decades ago. It would not be surprising if Syrah did well in the areas of the top Crus. Some producers have been planting trial plots of Syrah. Château des Jacques planted a hectare of Syrah in 2015, for producing a Vin de France. "The idea is not that we will use a lot of Syrah, it is just to be curious," says Cyril Chirouze. "Syrah is a beautiful variety, but Gamay is much better, it's more approachable," says Louis-Clément David-Beaupère. "We are a much more Burgundian producer than the Rhone valley, and Gamay is our identity."

The future is unclear. The practical difficulty is whether there is any alternative for the vineyards that are now producing Beaujolais Nouveau. Needless to say, these are not the best vineyards. Perhaps it's better that they produce Beaujolais Nouveau rather than join the lake of wine to be distilled, but the price is to devalue the reputation of the rest of Beaujolais. "Beaujolais Nouveau is one of the most incredible ideas of the twentieth century. People of my generation don't know that we have crus in Beaujolais—it's crazy," says Louis-Benoît Desvignes. Admittedly the crus vary from wines that are barely distinguishable from Beaujolais Villages to those that might be confused with reds from the Côte de Beaune, but the best are some of the few remaining undiscovered bargains from the region.

Jura

Jura-Savoie are usually lumped together as those regions which do not fit into Burgundy or the Rhône, but the vineyards are well separated and the connection is slight. The terroirs are different: Jura has rolling hills and Savoie has the grandeur of the mountains. The grape varieties are different. And there is little commonality of style. Savoie is dominated by indigenous varieties, mostly white. The Jura is caught between vinification of the Savagnin grape in an oxidative style producing wine akin to Sherry, contrasted with wines made in the modern style from Savagnin or Chardonnay. The Jura has generally been fairly obscure, with wine made by local producers on a relatively small scale, and not much interest from negociants from elsewhere, but recently there's been a small move into the region by producers from Burgundy.

About fifty miles east of Burgundy, the Jura is separated from the Côte d'Or by the valley of the Saône river. Vineyards in the Jura are more elevated (around 250-400m), on slopes that face west or southwest. Soils are clay and limestone, with outbreaks of marl (lime-rich mud). There is more clay in the Jura than in Burgundy, because when the massif of the Jura advanced towards Burgundy, clay was pushed up to the surface at the base of the foothills, whereas in Burgundy it remains underground. Cooler than Burgundy, and with more rain, the climate is marginal for wine growing.

Côtes de Jura is the general AOP for the whole region; within it the Arbois AOP is far larger than the small AOPs of Château-Chalon (this is the name of the AOP not a producer) and l'Etoile. There is also a tiny appellation of Arbois-Pupillin, just 300 ha on steep slopes above the village of Pupillin. In addition, there are two AOPs for specific wine styles: Crémant de Jura and Macvin (a sweet vin de liqueur made by adding spirits to stop fermentation at an early point).

In steady decline ever since phylloxera, when there were around 20,000 ha of vineyards, plantings in the Jura have now stabilized at under 2,000 ha, with almost all vineyards in one of the AOPs. Only five grape varieties are allowed in the AOPs: Chardonnay and Savagnin for the whites; and Poulsard, Trousseau, and Pinot Noir for the blacks. The trend is towards increasing production of white wines, which today are about two thirds of production (including sparkling as well as still wines).

Reflecting the symmetry with Burgundy across the Saône valley, Chardonnay is the predominant variety, accounting for about half of all plantings. It is not a newcomer here, having been grown for several centuries under a variety of local names. "People say, oh, now you are making Chardonnay in the Jura, but Chardonnay has been grown here for a very long time—some speak of the fourteenth century," says Stéphane Tissot. Yet in terms of stylistic imperatives, it is Savagnin that makes the running.

The local myth is that Savagnin was imported from Tokaji in Hungary in the Middle Ages. In fact, its origins are in the other direction, as it is the same variety as Gewürztraminer in Alsace, yet in the Jura it gives a wine with pronounced savory quality, rather than the floral perfume of Gewürztraminer. Essentially Savagnin is a nonaromatic variant and Gewürztraminer is an aromatic variant of

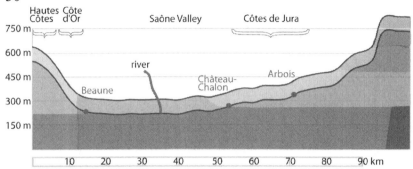

The southeast-facing slope of the Côte d'Or is separated from the southwest-facing slopes of the Jura by the valley of the Saône.

the variety. Savagnin or Chardonnay show a similar savory thread, as do wines blended from the two varieties.

It seems that the Jura has suddenly been discovered for the unusual character of its wines. "Five years ago it was easy to buy vines here, now it's difficult, the wines are having a great success and people don't want to sell," says Jacques Duvivier, who has come to Arbois to run the Marquis d'Angerville's expansion from Volnay into the Jura. "In the Jura we have specific soils and specific varieties, and we have to show that. The Jura is successful because it is original."

The Jura's claim to fame comes from its oxidative style of wines, almost unique in France. (Similar techniques are used in Gaillac for its *vin de voile*). Traditional winemaking used old barriques, but did not fill them completely or top up to compensate for loss by evaporation. The result is that a layer of yeast, known locally as the *voile* (veil), grows on the surface of the wine. Producers are quick to tell you that the yeasts aren't the same as those involved in the formation of flor on fino Sherry, but the principle is the same, and the results are similar. (Of course, Sherry is fortified but the Jura wines are natural, although evaporation during maturation can increase alcohol to a similar level.)

The layer of yeast is thinner in the Jura, and more gray in hue. It protects the maturing wine from becoming oxidized to vinegar, and contributes a distinctive aroma and flavor. The wine has a taut, savory quality with distinct dryness on the finish (because the yeasts consume glycerol). The main aromatic characteristics are the production of acetaldehyde (an oxidized product of ethanol), which

The traditional style in the Jura allows wine to mature in barriques that are not topped up. Yeast grow on the surface of the wine to form a voile (as seen here in a white layer about an inch deep).

gives a faintly nutty character, and sotolon, an aromatic, spicy compound that contributes curry-like notes. In fact, sotolon is also a natural product of the fenugreek plant, whose seeds are used in Madras curry.

The antithesis of the modern trend to fruit-driven wines, the oxidative style is an acquired taste that has been going out of fashion. As a result, most producers now also make wines in a modern, which is to say non-oxidative, style. The most common term used to describe these wines is *ouillé* (from ouillage, meaning topping-up). Wines in the oxidative style are most often described as traditional or *vinifié sur voile* (or sometimes *typé*). The distinction is a recent development: "The production of wines in the ouillé style at Château-Chalon started only around 1990," says Jean Berthet-Bondet, one of the leading producers. Some old-line producers have eschewed the ouillé style, but it's a sign of the times that Laurent Macle, from one of the most traditional producers in Château-Chalon, produced his first ouillé wine in 2007. It's only four barrels, but a source of argument as Laurent's father does not approve. "He will never be convinced," says Laurent, who believes this may be the true expression of terroir. "People confuse terroir with the taste of Vin Jaune (vinifié sur voile), but it's the aging that gives the wine its flavor."

The most fascinating aspect of the Jura is a certain sense of convergence between the oxidized and ouillé styles, and between Chardonnay and Savagnin. Even in the ouillé style, Chardonnay sometimes takes on a more savory quality, faintly reminiscent of Savagnin in its oxidized style. Walking in the vineyards, I was convinced I could smell fenugreek on the air. But it's more likely that the presence of both types of wine in the same cellar is responsible.

A tasting with Stéphane Tissot at Domaine André & Mireille Tissot provided an interesting comparison. The Traminer and Savagnin cuvées come from the same vines, but the names of the cuvées indicate different types of vinification. Traminer is nonoxidative, but Savagnin has 30 months under voile. Even the first shows some savory influences, but they are much stronger in the second. One seems more like an extreme example of the other, rather than completely different.

Wines in the oxidative style go back at least to the eighteenth century, and the epitome of the style is Vin Jaune, which matures in barrique under a voile for six years. Vin Jaune comes exclusively from Savagnin. For most appellations it is one of several wine styles that can be produced, but Château-Chalon produces only Vin Jaune, and is usually considered to provide its peak expression. (Any other wine produced from vineyards within Château-Chalon must be labeled Côtes de Jura.)

"Château-Chalon is the grand cru of Vin Jaune. You don't have the right to produce Château-Chalon every vintage. A commission meets to decide whether to allow the appellation each year," explains Jean-François Bourdy, who has strong views about the roles of the varieties. "The tradition here—for more than fifty years—is that Chardonnay makes the best white wines. Savagnin makes Vin Jaune."

Emphasizing the expensive nature of its production, Vin Jaune is sold in an unusual 62 cl. bottle (supposedly to represent what is left after evaporation of a liter of wine from the harvest). Vin Jaune has an intensity that matches a top fino Sherry, but has a slightly different aroma and flavor spectrum, if anything deeper and more savory.

It would be a mistake to regard the difference between the traditional and ouillé styles as a polarizing influence: they are more the extremes of a continuum. Modernism is perhaps defined by Ganevat, who at the southern tip of the Jura is almost completely devoted to the ouillé style; his Chardonnays show a minerality and

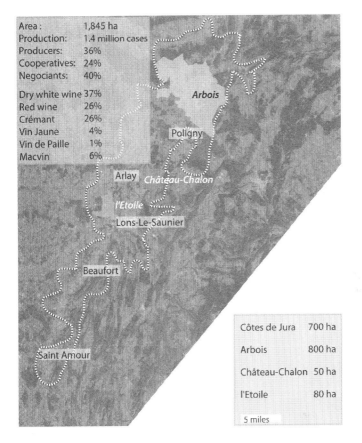

Area:	1,845 ha
Production:	1.4 million cases
Producers:	36%
Cooperatives:	24%
Negociants:	40%
Dry white wine	37%
Red wine	26%
Crémant	26%
Vin Jaune	4%
Vin de Paille	1%
Macvin	6%

Arbois

Poligny

Arlay Château-Chalon

l'Etoile

Lons-Le-Saunier

Beaufort

Saint Amour

Côtes de Jura	700 ha
Arbois	800 ha
Château-Chalon	50 ha
l'Etoile	80 ha

5 miles

The individual appellations of Arbois, Château-Chalon, and l'Etoile are relatively compact, but the Côtes de Jura extends over 50 miles.

freshness reminiscent of Chablis. At the center are producers like Stéphane Tissot, making wines in both styles, but with oxidized wines varying from relatively brief exposure to the full reign of Vin Jaune. Traditional producer Jacques Puffeney made a Chardonnay in a style that shows herbs and spices of the garrigue with a touch of fenugreek leading into a savory palate, but which is more of a halfway house between traditional and ouillé as it doesn't have the madeirized quality of Vin Jaune.

Some producers now make a halfway style, typically by blending Chardonnay produced under ouillé conditions with a smaller proportion of Savagnin produced under voile. There are different

Château-Chalon is located at a high point on a plateau overlooking the vineyards of the appellation down below. Soils of blue marl retain heat, and the vineyards are protected from the wind by south-southwest exposure.

stories about the origins of this approach, but it seems to be an attempt to introducing the oxidative style in a more subtle manner.

The reds in the Jura are less interesting than the whites. They are split between Pinot Noir and the local varieties Poulsard and Trousseau. The main change in the past few decades is an increase in Pinot Noir from almost negligible to around a third of black plantings. (However, Pinot Noir is not a newcomer: in the eighteenth century it was the second most planted variety.) Poulsard (also called Plousard locally) is by far the most important, representing more than three quarters of the black plantings (roughly a quarter of all plantings).

Poulsard and Trousseau are somewhat rustic in a light style. Poulsard has such a light, thin skin that it's often taken for rosé. It's relatively rare for Pinot Noir to acquire really enough concentration, although some of the wines from the glorious 2009 vintage could be mistaken for coming from the environs of Beaune. This might be an indication that the Jura would be a good place for Pinot Noir if global warming continues, although of course the presence of more clay and less limestone is problematic in that regard. I'm not sure I see much purpose in blending the varieties: it doesn't give the Poul-

Reference Wines for Jura	
Chardonnay, ouillé	Domaine Ganevat, Les Chalasses
Savagnin, ouillé	Domaine André & Mireille Tissot, Arbois (Traminer)
Chardonnay, traditional	Domaine Jacques Puffeney, Arbois
Savagnin, traditional	Domaine André & Mireille Tissot, Arbois (Savagnin)
Trousseau	Domaine Jacques Puffeney, Les Berangères
Vin Jaune	Domaine Berthet-Bondet, Château-Chalon
Vin de Paille	Domaine Jean Bourdy, Côtes de Jura

sard or Trousseau more refinement, nor does it round out the Pinot Noir.

The wines of Jacques Puffeney, among the most subtle of the appellation, illustrate the differences between the black varieties. The Pinot Noir is delicate, but with a touch of austerity, somewhat in the direction of a red Sancerre, but tighter. Trousseau has more weight and depth, and although many Trousseau wines from the Jura can seem on the rustic side, Puffeney's Les Bérangères, with its slightly darker color and high alcohol, demonstrates the full potential of the variety for pulling off a richness that Pinot Noir cannot quite achieve in this environment. But Puffeney is recognized as the master of Trousseau.

A significant part of the Jura's production is Crémant, mostly made from Chardonnay, but some black grapes are also used. While there are exceptions, the Crémant is not usually especially interesting, and its main significance may be that it improves the quality of the still wines by using up grapes that are just short of full ripeness.

Even aside from its unique Vin Jaune, the Jura offers an unusual alternative to the monotony of simple fruit-driven wines; traditional or ouillé, Chardonnay or Savagnin, these are some of the more distinctive wines of France.

Savoie

It's hard to know what to expect of the wines of Savoie. Under the Alps, stretching from Grenoble to Geneva, it's far from obvious that this is a natural area for wine, yet production predates the Romans. Savoie became part of France only in 1860, so its grape varieties and traditions are distinct. Historically vines were planted all the way from the valleys up to around 1,000m of elevation. At the time of phylloxera, there were about 20,000 hectares of vineyards; since a recovery in the first two decades of the twentieth century, the planted area has been falling steadily, down today to little more than 2,000 ha. Almost all is in Savoie itself, with little left in Haut Savoie (Savoie is the southern half, and Haut Savoie is the northern half, of the former kingdom of Savoy, before it was annexed by France).

The most important vineyards are south of Chambéry, along the gorge of Chambéry or running along the Combe de Savoie, a striking 25-mile long valley bounded by the massive mountains that run on an axis from Chambéry through Aix-les-Bains and Annécy. On the gorge of Chambéry, Les Abymes and Apremont face the vineyards across the Combe de Savoie, where Saint-Jeoire-Prieuré, Chignin, Montmélian, Arbin and Cruet, look towards the mountains.

Proximity to the mountains, and elevation of vineyards, make this distinctly cool climate territory, comparable to Alsace or the Loire. Most of the wine is white, and falls under the AOPs of Vin de Savoie or Roussette de Savoie (which is monovarietal Roussette from anywhere in the region). In addition to the 90% of production labeled as Vin de Savoie, there are fifteen crus, whose individual names can be appended to the Vin de Savoie AOP, which is really far too many separate appellations. The most important crus in terms of both quantity and reputation are Les Abymes and Apremont. Roussette de Savoie has four crus that can be appended to its name. There is a small amount of production under AOP Seyssel. There's also the IGP Allobrogies, which covers the whole area with a generally similar set of grape varieties. The fact, however, is that the variety, or the blend of varieties, is probably the most important factor in determining style.

Altogether there are 23 grape varieties in Savoie. The main white variety is Jacquère, which accounts for half of all plantings, and is supposed to have been imported into the region in the thir-

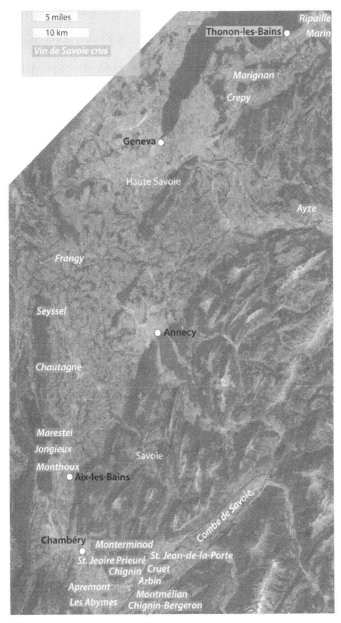

The wines of Savoie come from three separate areas: the remaining vineyards of Haut Savoie are near Lake Geneva; in the center are vineyards to the north of Aix-les-Bains; and the main group of vineyards is clustered to the south of Chambéry.

Mont Granier looms over the vineyards of Chignin. Courtesy Savoie-Mont Blanc.

teenth century. It's a late-ripening, productive variety; in fact yields up to 78 hl/ha are allowed for the regional AOP, and between 65-75 hl/ha for the crus. Vins de Savoie are typically blends based on Jacquère; the major blending varieties are Chasselas, Roussanne, and Chardonnay. There are more specific assemblages in some of the crus. Les Abymes must be 80% Jacquère, and Apremont is exclusively Jacquère, as is Chignin; but Chignin-Bergeron is exclusively Roussanne. Crépy is exclusively Chasselas. The second most important white variety, Roussette, also known as Altesse, is mostly vinified as a monovarietal for the AOP Roussette de Savoie and its crus.

Red wine is only a quarter of production, split between Gamay (probably introduced after phylloxera) and Mondeuse, an indigenous variety, with origins related to Syrah. Another indigenous variety called Persan is also found. Mondeuse is especially prominent in the Combe de Savoie, and notably in the crus Arbin and Saint-Jean-de-la-Porte. It gives a slightly astringent, peppery wine, quite tannic.

The best wines can be intriguingly different, and could hardly be more distinct from the modern "international" style, but some-

Reference Wines for Savoie	
Roussette de Savoie	Domaine du Prieuré Saint Christophe
Vin de Savoie, Arbin	Domain Louis Magnin, Tout un Monde
Chignin-Bergeron	Domaine Louis Magnin, Grand Orgue

times lack flavor interest. The nutty notes of Jacquère at its best can be attractive; the Roussanne of Chignin-Bergeron makes a fresher impression. The reds can be a bit rustic. Mondeuse is the most distinctive, but when very young it tends to show a fairly dull flavor spectrum, and it's hard for it to rise above the general level of rusticity, although Louis Magnin's top cuvées can become elegant with age.

Visiting the Region

Côte Chalonnaise

This is quite an accessible region, with the main road running straight down from the southernmost part of the Côte d'Or. It would be easy to visit producers in all the appellations in the same day. Mercurey is the main town. Like the Côte d'Or, larger producers have tasting rooms that are open with no appointment required, but it is a good idea to call ahead to smaller producers, where the owner may be the only person available to show visitors around.

Mâcon and Beaujolais

The Mâconnais runs directly into Beaujolais. The most interesting producers in Mâcon are in its southern part, and the most interesting producers in Beaujolais are in its northern part, so it is possible to combine visits to the two regions. Mâcon is the largest town in the area, but 30-45 minutes away from the producers. Anywhere between Pouilly Fuissé and Villié Morgon is good base for visiting producers. Roads tend to twist and turn through the hills, so it's easy to get lost, which makes it a good idea to allow plenty of time between appointments in different villages. While some producers have tasting rooms that are open to visitors, the region is less tourist-oriented than the Côte d'Or, and it's a good idea to make appointments almost everywhere.

40

The Jura

The Jura is more spread out than it seems, but most producers can be accessed from one of the two main towns, Château-Chalon and Arbois. In a really elevated position, Château-Chalon is one of the sights of the region in its own right. Arbois is a lively little town, with many producers represented by tasting rooms that are open all day. Don't be surprised to be offered red wines to taste before white, because the whites are so aromatic. "You won't be able to taste the reds after the Savagnin," is a common view.

Vintages

Chalonnaise and Mâcon

Vintages are generally similar to the Côte de Beaune, but of course the wines are not so long-lived. Most wines of the Côte Chalonnaise should be drunk within five years, and it's an exceptional Mâcon that will last longer than, say, three years, although some Pouilly Fuissés age well.

2015	***	Lovely vintage for reds, very generous, whites are supple and flavorful.
2014	**	The wines are lively, with good weight and freshness.
2013		Cold growing season was difficult, but some improvement in September allowed decent harvest for wines that will be good rather than great.
2012	*	Erratic conditions led to low yields of both reds and whites, but quality is surprisingly good.
2011		Difficulties in getting to ripeness make this the least successful vintage of the decade to date.
2010	**	Reds are tight. Whites show good acidity in a leaner style than 2009
2009	***	Reds and whites are both rich, ripe and opulent.
2008		Difficult vintage with problems of rain and humidity. Reds show high acidity, whites are on the fresh side.
2007		Growing season was too wet, reds suffered from problems with humidity, whites are better but on the acid side.

2006	*	Not a generous vintage, both whites and reds tended to be somewhat tight
2005	***	A top vintage with general tendency to opulence in both reds and whites.
2004	*	Both reds and whites are on the lighter, more acid side, and there are not many of interest today.
2003		Reds tended to be cooked from the outset. The heat was too much for the whites, which tended to be flabby.
2002	**	Reds are rich but well structured. Whites tended to show opulence but now too old.

Beaujolais

With almost all Beaujolais intended for immediate consumption, vintages are usually simply a guide as to whether or not to buy the current release. Even for the crus, little is available on the market beyond the last two or three years, but because there have been some unusually fine years lately, with exceptional potential for aging for the crus, there's more interest than usual. Very few wines are worth keeping more than a decade, however, and recommendations for longevity really apply only to the top crus, Moulin-à-Vent, Morgon, Fleurie, and perhaps Juliénas.

Vintage conditions have shown more extreme swings, with crops enormously reduced by hail in 2016 and 2017. "Normal years don't exist any more," says Jean-Louis Dutraive, whose vineyards were ravaged by a hailstorm both years. Two great vintages within a decade's span is unusual, but first 2009 and then 2015 produced wines with great generosity. "In all of Beaujolais, 2015 is a more southern style, but the grapes were ripe and there was good acidity and balance with potential to age," says Mee Godard.

2016	*	A restrained vintage, fresh from the Villages, tight from the Crus, but yields reduced by hail.
2015	***	A generous vintage, the richest and best rounded since 2009. Wines are ripe, round, and attractive.
2014		A cool August created problems but was followed by an Indian summer. However, many wines have rather high lev-

		els of acidity and appear a little tight rather than generous.
2013		A difficult vintage, with a cold wet start to the season, but good September. Fruits are light and pleasant, but the danger is that they will be overtaken by the acidity.
2012	**	"2012 is the smallest vintage I have experienced, with hail and rain early, but the weather became sunny from mid August. Harvest started from September 12; the quantity was not there but the quality was definitely there," says Georges Duboeuf.
2011	**	This is often considered to be as good as 2009, although it hasn't attracted the same attention; but the best wines will age well, as they have good concentration and structure.
2010	**	Another very good year, which would have been classic if not following 2009. There's a lot of fruit here, although not as opulent as 2009.
2009	***	"2009 is the best vintage I have known in my life. We had (all the) berries in perfect condition which I have never seen before," says Georges Duboeuf. The top crus will last for several years yet.
2008		A slow, late vintage that called for a lot of selection; wines were relatively short lived.
2007	*	A nice vintage, small but with good quality.
2006		Rather a mixed vintage, generally with average results.
2005	***	A very good year, as in Burgundy; overshadowed in the decade only by 2009.
2004	*	A normal vintage was a relief after the excessive heat of the previous year.

Profiles of Estates

Ratings

*** Excellent producers defining the very best of the appellation
 ** Top producers whose wines typify the appellation
  * Very good producers making wines of character that rarely disappoint

Symbols

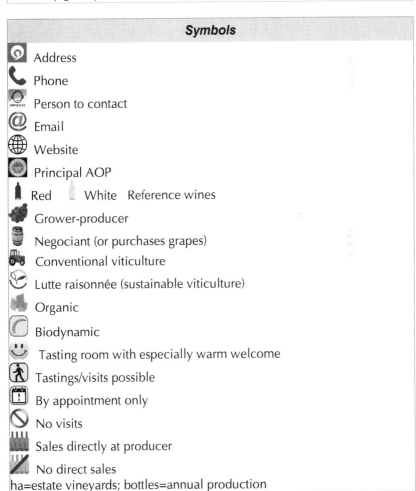

Address

Phone

Person to contact

@ Email

Website

Principal AOP

Red   White   Reference wines

Grower-producer

Negociant (or purchases grapes)

Conventional viticulture

Lutte raisonnée (sustainable viticulture)

Organic

Biodynamic

Tasting room with especially warm welcome

Tastings/visits possible

By appointment only

No visits

Sales directly at producer

No direct sales

ha=estate vineyards; bottles=annual production

Chalonnaise

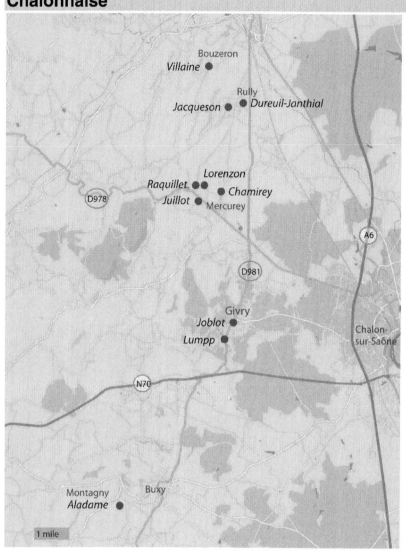

Domaine Stéphane Aladame

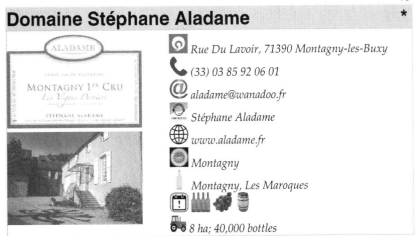

Rue Du Lavoir, 71390 Montagny-les-Buxy

(33) 03 85 92 06 01

aladame@wanadoo.fr

Stéphane Aladame

www.aladame.fr

Montagny

Montagny, Les Maroques

8 ha; 40,000 bottles

The domain is located in a group of old buildings around a courtyard, just above the town of Montagny. "I created the domain in 1992 when I bought 2.5 ha from a vigneron who was retiring. I was eighteen at the time," recollects Stéphane Aladame. Since then, it's been built up slowly to its present size, and now there are six cuvées of Montagny premier cru plus a Crémant. There are no vines in Montagny village, but Stéphane has a negociant activity to produce Montagny AOP.

Cuvée Decouverte is an assemblage of premier crus from young vines (less than 20 years old), vinified in cuve for 10 months, with some lees. Cuvée Selection Vieilles Vignes comes from four different premier cru parcels (older than 40 years), and is matured 60% in oak with 10% new. Most of the premier crus are matured in proportions of old barriques and cuve, but the premier crus with the oldest vines (Les Coères at 45 years and Les Burnins at 90 years) are matured exclusively in old barriques.

The style tends to elegance, with smooth fruits, and a characteristic catch of lime at the end, reflecting the emphasis on maintaining freshness and precision. "I don't look for wines with too much maturity, too heavy. I harvest relatively early and want to keep acidity. I may have a degree less of alcohol, usually it's 12.5-13%. I look for minerality rather than richness," Stéphane says. Fruit concentration and the sense of texture resulting from oak exposure intensify going up the hierarchy.

Château de Chamirey ∗

Rue du Château, 71640 Mercurey

(33) 03 85 45 21 61

contact@domaines-devillard.com

Amaury Devillard

www.chamirey.com

Mercurey

Mercurey, Clos du Roi

Mercurey, en Pierrelet

37 ha; 200,000 bottles

The vineyards of this estate are exclusively in Mercurey, concentrated around the rather splendid château, which was added to the estate two generations ago in 1931. The modern winery has a spacious tasting room. The fifth generation of the Devillard family run the estate today. Across from the château is a modern winery, with a spacious tasting room and restaurant. Vineyards are two thirds black to one third white, with 15 ha in premier crus. The whites are fruit-driven and nicely rounded, very attractive for short or mid-term drinking, but not likely to be especially long-lived.

The village wine is matured in 400 liter casks to preserve its minerality, with no new oak; the top white is a premier cru, the monopole La Mission, which is aged for 15 months in barriques with one third new oak. The red Mercurey comes from several plots, six from the village AOP, and includes two from premier crus, to increase quality, which has an influence especially in cooler years. Premier cru Ruelles is a monopole, but the top red is Les Cinq, a blend of the best lots from each of the five premier crus (production is small, only 1,900 bottles in 2010).

All wines, especially the reds, have evident notes of ripeness approaching over-ripeness, so it was not a surprise to hear that, "We are always the last in Mercurey to harvest, we pick very late" (for both reds and whites). In addition to Château de Chamirey, the Devillards own Domaine de Perdrix in Nuits St. Georges, and Domaine de la Ferté just to the south in Givry.

Domaine Vincent Dureuil-Janthial ★★★

Rue De La Buisserolle, 71150 Rully

(33) 03 85 87 26 32

vincent.dureuil@wanadoo.fr

Vincent Dureuil

dureuiljanthial-vins.com

Rully

Rully, Maizières

Rully, Margotés

20 ha; 100,000 bottles

The range and quality of wines justify this estate's reputation as the most important domain in Rully. At the back of the town, a tasting room in a charming house on one side of the street is run by Vincent's father, and a practical winery, more or less a warehouse, extends along the opposite side of the street. The domain was started by Vincent's grandfather; Vincent took over twenty years ago when he was 24.

The holdings are a bit complicated: Vincent has 3 ha in his own name, his father has some, his father-in-law has 1 ha (premier cru in Nuits St. Georges), and 6 ha are rented on long term contracts. "There's no land for sale in Rully, so it's impossible to buy more vineyards," Vincent explains. Vineyards are organic, because "biodynamic is just too expensive for the Côte Chalonnaise."

The 16 cuvées come mostly from Rully, with many premier crus, which we tasted not according to terroirs, but in order of vine age, which Vincent evidently views as a more important determinant of quality. The oldest vineyard is in Meix Cadots (the Vieilles Vignes cuvée, planted in 1920, now giving yields of 30 hl/ha.) "For the money it would be better to plant new vines and get 55 hl/ha, but it's four generations of work," Vincent says ruefully. The style shows minerality and precision. The whites are the glory of the domain, at their best a lesser man's Puligny. Reds show the limitations of the Chalonnaise, but with characteristic precision for Rully and earthy breadth for Mercurey.

Maison Paul et Marie Jacqueson ✱

📍 *5, Rue De Chèvremont, 71150 Rully*

📞 *(33) 03 85 91 25 91*

@ *marie.jacqueson@wanadoo.fr*

👤 *Paul & Marie Jacqueson*

🌐 *www.domainejacqueson.fr*

🔲 *Rully*

🏛 *Rully, Cloux*

🍾 *Rully, Margotés*

🚜 *14 ha; 80,000 bottles*

The long building that dominates the street was built in 2013; previously the domain was in much smaller space across the road. Marie Jacqueson's grandfather started the domain in 1946 with some vines from his parents. He had another job, working for a domain in Mercurey, but slowly he bought vines. Her father took over in 1972, and Marie took over in 2006. Vineyards continue to be added, and the domain has now almost doubled in size from when Marie's father started.

The domain is principally in Rully but also has some Bouzeron and Mercurey. Overall it is 60% white. There are 18 different cuvées from Bourgogne Aligoté through Rully premier cru in whites and reds, and a Passetoutgrains—"We have everything," Marie says. "Our specialty with the Bouzeron is the élevage of Aligoté entirely in fûts (but no new wood, of course)."

The heart of the domain lies in the Rully premier crus, Grésigny (with the oldest vines of the domain, planted by Marie's grandfather 60 years ago), La Pucelle, Raclot, and Les Cordères in white, and Les Naugues and Les Cloux in red. "All the white Rully premier crus are treated the same way and have 20% new oak. Any differences are due to terroir," Marie says. For reds there is complete destemming and 25% new oak. The house style with whites is quite fat, more stone fruits than citrus, with a texture on the palate approaching the style of the Côte d'Or. Reds can be tight at first, then broaden and become earthy after a year or so.

Domaine Joblot ∗

◎ *4, Rue Pasteur, 71640 Givry*

📞 *(33) 03 85 44 30 77*

@ *domaine.joblot@orange.fr*

✉ *Juliettte Joblot*

🌐 *www.domainejoblot.com*

◉ *Givry*

🍾 *Givry, Cellier aux Moines*

🚫 🏭 🍇

🚜 *14 ha; 65,000 bottles*

Run by brothers Jean-Marc and Vincent Joblot, this domain produces mostly red wine from Givry, with a small proportion of white. Jean-Marc's daughter Juliette is now taking over as winemaker; she is also involved with Domaine Lienhardt in Comblanchien, run by her partner Antoine Lienhardt. Functioning more or less out of the family property, Joblot is widely considered to be a point of reference for the appellation.

Vineyards in the northern part of Givry are three quarters in premier crus, the best of which are Clos du Cellier aux Moines (the oldest known vineyard in Givry) and Clos de la Servoisine. There are 8 cuvées altogether, 3 white and 5 red (including one red and one white Givry AOP; the rest are premier cru). One unusual feature here is that date of harvest is determined by acidity levels, so the wines have not succumbed to the fashion for increasing ripeness or over-ripeness. With painstaking viticulture, yields are kept low and there is intense selection of grapes at harvest. Grapes are destemmed, and there is long cool maceration before fermentation.

There's extensive use of new oak, but the brothers are very fussy about the extent of toast (it should not be too much); barrels come from a long-standing relationship with François Frères. Vinification is the same for all wines, with the stated aim of minimal intervention to ensure that differences between the cuvées are due solely to terroir. Oak can be evident in young wines, so do not try to drink before, say, three years.

Domaine Michel Juillot ★

2006

Domaine Michel Juillot

Mercurey

APPELLATION MERCUREY CONTROLÉE
VIN DE BOURGOGNE
PRODUCE OF FRANCE

LAURENT JUILLOT VITICULTEUR A MERCUREY S&L FRANCE

59, Grande Rue, 71640 Mercurey

(33) 03 85 98 99 89

infos@domaine-michel-juillot.fr

Laurent Juillot

www.domaine-michel-juillot.fr

Mercurey

Mercurey, Clos Tonnerre

Mercurey, Vignes de Maillonge

33 ha; 180,000 bottles

Located on the main road through Mercurey, the tasting room of this domain seems continually thronged with visitors. The domain is now in its fourth generation, under Laurent Juillot since 1988 (although his father, Michel, a well known character in the town, remains in evidence). It's expanded greatly under the last two generations, from 6 ha when Michel took it over in 1963.

Two thirds of the vineyards are in Mercurey, mostly red, with a significant proportion in premier crus; in addition there are holdings in Rully and Bourgogne, and also some in Aloxe-Corton and Corton. The range is wide, but the real interest here is to compare the premier crus, vinified in the same way for either whites or reds, to demonstrate terroir. Vinification is traditional, with élevage in barriques for 12 months for whites and 16-18 months for reds. For whites, new oak (25%) is used only for the three premier crus; for reds, new oak varies from 15% for the Mercurey to 35% for the five premier crus. The barriques come mostly from the Vosges. There's an unusual policy of holding stocks from older vintages.

The reds tend to start out a little hard, which is typical of Mercurey, but soften in an earthy direction after a couple of years; they tend to peak around five or six years after the vintage. The whites in my view tend to be more successful; the Mercurey AOP is a bit straightforward in its flavor spectrum, but the premier crus show a nice sense of reserve to the stone and citrus fruits.

Domaine Bruno Lorenzon

Carline

par

L■renzon
Mercurey.France

Rue du Reu, 71640 Mercurey

(33) 03 85 45 13 51

contact@domainelorenzon.com

Bruno Lorenzon

www.domainelorenzon.com

Mercurey

Mercurey, Les Champs Martin

5 ha; 20,000 bottles

In a back street of Mercurey, the domain itself has a somewhat dilapidated appearance; at the main entrance there's a notice directing you to the office around the back, which as likely as not will be closed also. Don't expect to be able to visit, with or without an appointment. Perhaps that is because Bruno Lorenzon is in the vineyards, following up on his favorite saying, "Great berries are 90% of the work."

This small domain is now in its third generation under Bruno, who took over in 1997, after prior experience in foreign countries (he has made wine in South Africa and New Zealand as a consultant), and a stint with the tonnellerie in Mercurey (with whom he remains associated). Bruno runs the domain together with his sister Carline. Barriques come from the tonnellerie (there is 20-40% new wood for whites and 15-40% for reds). Élevage lasts from 9 to 18 months.

Vineyards are almost exclusively in Mercurey, almost all in premier crus, with 4 ha of red and 1 ha of white (including 6 red and 5 white premier crus); there are also Montagny and Corton Charlemagne. The main holding is a large block (3.7 ha) in the center of the steep limestone slope of the Champs Martin premier cru. This is planted with both Pinot Noir and Chardonnay. The style is modern, tending to good color and extraction. It reaches its peak in the vieilles vignes cuvée Carline from Champs Martin (aged for 19 months in 40% new oak), which tends to have more power rather than greater typicity compared with the regular cuvée.

Domaine François Lumpp   *

36, Avenue De Mortières, Le Pied Du Clou, 71640 Givry

(33) 03 85 44 45 57

domaine@francoislumpp.com

Isabelle & François Lumpp

www.francoislumpp.com

Givry

9 ha; 45,000 bottles

Created when François, who had been making wine in Givry since 1977, split from his brother at the family domain in 1991 to create his own domain, this is considered to be one of the most reliable domains in Givry. (His brother's domain is Vincent Lumpp.) It is headquartered in a workmanlike building on the main road through town. Starting with 3.5 ha, the domain has slowly expanded. Today there are 7.5 ha of red and 2 ha of white.

The vineyards are exclusively in Givry; there's a village white cuvée and premier cru, and six red premier crus. In fact, the majority of production is in premier crus. François and Isabelle Lumpp have replanted most of their vineyards with closer spacing to reduce yields (using a really dense 11,000 vines per hectare, with vines coming by selection massale from the Côte d'Or). The stated aim is to harvest at "just ripe," rather than over-ripe. The various premier crus are distinguished by position on the slope, with Pied de Clou at the bottom, next to the winery, Crausot at the top, and the best, La Vigne Rouge and Clos du Cras Long, coming from mid-slope. The 2 ha of Vigne Rouge are the most recent acquisition of the estate (in 2007).

New oak barriques can be found in the cellar, up to about 30%, but the aim is that the taste of oak should not be evident in the wine. Following plantings in Givry, the focus is on reds, but the domain has an equally high reputation for its whites. Reception can be on the chilly side for visitors.

Domaine François Raquillet

FRANÇOIS RAQUILLET

MERCUREY 1ᵉʳ CRU
Appellation Mercurey 1ᵉʳ Cru Contrôlée
LES VASÉES

———— 2011 ————

○ *19, Rue De Jamproyes, 71640 Mercurey*

☎ *(33) 03 85 45 14 61*

@ *francoisraquillet@club-internet.fr*

○ *François Raquillet*

⊕ *www.domaine-raquillet.com*

◉ *Mercurey*

▮ *Mercurey, Les Veleys*

▮ *Mercurey, Les Velley*

🚜 *10 ha; 50,000 bottles*

François Raquillet is proud of being the eleventh generation in a line of vignerons passing from father to son since the seventeenth century. The domain was formally established in 1963, and François joined his father in 1984; he took over together with his wife Emmanuelle in 1990. By reducing yields (by removing buds at bud break) and modernizing vinification, in particular increasing the emphasis on the quality of oak barrels (using barriques for reds, and 500 liter barrels for whites, with new oak now up to 30%), François revitalized the domain, which is now considered a reference point for Mercurey.

Holdings are closely focused on the appellation, with vieilles vignes village level white and red, and then a lieu-dit and premier cru white, and four premier cru reds. The estate vineyards in Mercurey have 8 ha of Pinot Noir and 2 ha of Chardonnay, with an average vine age of 35 years. They are supplemented with purchases of grapes from vineyards that François harvests himself, extending the range to a Bourgogne red, and white Rully premier cru and Meursault. After sorting, reds are fermented in concrete, whites in the 500 liter barrels, with little battonage. Élevage lasts a year, longer for the top premier crus. The red premier crus can show unusual minerality and precision for Mercurey. Although the domaine nominally welcomes visits, in practice visitors are likely to find a notice redirecting them to the communal tasting room in the town if they want to try the wines.

Domaine Aubert et Pamela De Villaine   *

DOMAINE A. ET P. DE VILLAINE
Propriétaire à Bouzeron

Bouzeron

Appellation Bouzeron Contrôlée

Mis en Bouteille au Domaine
12.5 % vol   *Vin de Bourgogne · Product of France*   750 ml

2, *Rue De La Fontaine, 71150 Bouzeron*

(33) 03 85 91 20 50

contact@de-villaine.com

Pierre De Benoist

www.de-villaine.com

Bouzeron

Mercurey, Les Montots

Bourgogne, Les Clous

23 ha; 110,000 bottles

In addition to running Domaine de la Romanée Conti, Aubert Villaine, together with his wife Pamela, makes wine at this domain in the Côte Chalonnaise. The Villaines purchased and revived the domain in the seventies, expanding it from its original 8 ha. The domain has been managed since 2000 by Aubert's nephew, Pierre de Benoist. Almost half of the domain's vineyards are in Bouzeron, planted with Aligoté Doré on the tops of the slopes; Chardonnay and Pinot Noir are planted lower. The Aligoté makes the Bouzeron appellation wine.

Aubert became one of the spokesmen for Aligoté when he was involved in obtaining appellation status for Bouzeron, and the domain wine is one of the flagships for the appellation, showing citrus fruits, sometimes a touch spicy, in a light and attractive style. The Chardonnay and Pinot Noir are the basis for the various Bourgogne Côte Chalonnaise cuvées: Les Clous and Les Clous Aimé in whites; Les Clous, La Fortune, and La Digoine in reds. There is also a white from Rully.

For the Bourgogne and Rully, the house style for Chardonnay shows as a delicious acidity balancing between citrus and stone fruits with a nicely textured finish: both the Les Clous and Les Clous Aimé are a cut above the usual generic Bourgogne Blanc. Among the reds, I prefer the Mercurey to the Bourgogne cuvées. The domain produced wine exclusively from the Côte Chalonnaise until a small parcel was purchased in Santenay in 2011.

Macon

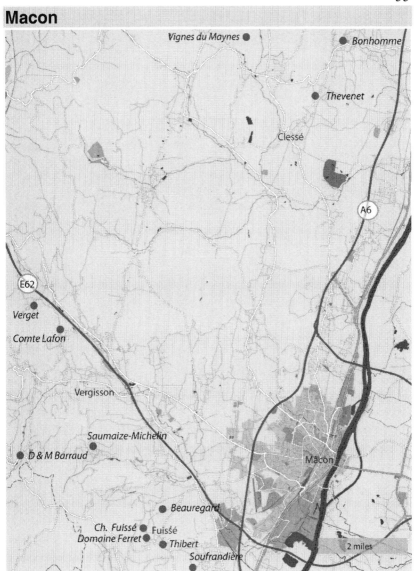

Vignes du Maynes ●

● Bonhomme

● Thevenet

Clessé

A6

E62

● Verget

● Comte Lafon

Vergisson

● Saumaize-Michelin

● D & M Barraud

Macon

● Beauregard

Ch. Fuissé ● Fuissé

Domaine Ferret ● ● Thibert

Soufrandière

2 miles

Domaine Daniel et Martine Barraud   *

Les Nembrets, 71960 Vergisson

(33) 03 85 35 84 25

contact@domainebarraud.com

Daniel Barraud

www.domainebarraud.com

Pouilly-Fuissé

Pouilly-Fuissé, en France

12 ha; 65,000 bottles

Although the Barrauds have had vineyards around Vergisson since 1890, the domain was effectively founded by Daniel and Martine Barraud. "We created all the buildings, our parents did not have any buildings, they were small growers" explains Martine. "My husband comes from a family of vignerons in Vergisson and he is the fourth generation. Today our son Julien and his sister are taking over. My husband has reached retirement age, but is still working.".

The domain has grown gradually over the years and has now officially become Daniel & Julien Barraud. It's located on the slope of the Roche de Vergisson, and is surrounded by vineyards. Daniel was just visible on his tractor in the vineyards when we arrived at the domain. Although the domain is small, the focus is on single vineyard wines, with no less than six cuvées from Pouilly-Fuissé, where vineyards are concentrated in Vergisson, but there are also three cuvées each from St. Véran and Mâcon.

The caves are quite modern, and Martine says, "here at this domain we have tradition and modernity. We hold to a very simple, traditional, method of working. My husband always says we are *agriculture des vignes*. Vinification is in barriques and demi-muids, with just a little new oak, 15-30% maximum (for the Vieilles Vignes cuvée)." Élevage lasts 10-15 months, and wines are bottled without fining or filtration.

Macon Chaintré is light and attractive. In St. Véran, en Creches is fruity from a southeast-facing vineyard, whereas Les Pommards comes from older vines (planted in 1963) on a northeast-facing slope, giving long hang time, and more presence on the palate. Alliance is the only blended cuvée in Pouilly Fuissé; the others all represent lieu-dits. "We've always treated the parcels individually, *nous sommes presque toute parcellaire*, we like the principle of showing terroir in each wine."

In Pouilly Fuissé, en France comes from a lieu-dit with thin soil on bedrock, and is a little rounder than the St. Vérans. La Verchère is the parcel of 60-year-old vines around the house, and is silkier. Les Crays comes from under the Roche de Vergisson; "this gives very small berries and concentrated wine with lots of finesse," says Martine. With a very fine texture, it has a greater sense of minerality, even salinity. La Roche is always the most mineral, coming from 35-year old vines growing at the highest altitudes; en Bulands comes from 80-year-old vines, and is always the last to be harvested, and the richest. Coming from four parcels of 35-60-year-old vines that are too small to vinify separately, Alliance has the same assemblage each year. It's more forceful than the individual cuvées but maintains the same light, airy style. The Pouilly Fuissés are a classic representation of the appellation.

Château de Beauregard ***

Beauregard, 71960 Fuissé

+33 (0)3 85 35 61 49

joseph.burrier@wanadoo.fr

Fréderic Marc Burrier

www.joseph-burrier.com

Pouilly-Fuissé

Pouilly-Fuissé, Vers Cras

46 ha; 380,000 bottles

One of the top domains—perhaps the top domain—in Pouilly-Fuissé, Château Beauregard occupies a cluster of old buildings a mile or so out of the town of Fuissé. Beauregard is the largest producer in Pouilly-Fuissé, and also has holdings in Beaujolais. "I feel like a true producer of South Burgundy, I do not see any difference between Beaujolais and here," says Frédéric-Marc Burrier, who is president of the growers association. In that capacity, he is deeply committed to the development of premier crus for the appellation, and his own wines certainly reflect nuances of terroir. There are two communal wines coming from younger and older vines, and then a series of eight single vineyard wines representing different *climats*.

These are probably the most ageworthy wines in Pouilly-Fuissé, with the top cuvées maturing for thirty years or so. Winemaking is traditional. "There has been no change here, I am making wines just like my father and grandfather," says Frédéric-Marc. "I am the last to use a mechanical press," he adds, explaining that in his opinion the excessive clarity achieved by pneumatic presses can cause early aging. Wines are fermented in barrique, stay in cask for a year, and are racked only at the end. The same 10-15% new oak is used for all cuvées. Beauregard is known as a white wine producer, but the reds from the top crus of Beaujolais have an unusual refinement and elegance that lifts them well above the usual impression of Gamay.

Domaine André Bonhomme

Rue Jean Large, 71260 Viré

(33) 03 85 33 11 86

earl.bonhomme.andre@terre-net.fr

Aurelia Bonhomme

www.vireclessebonhomme.fr

Viré-Clessé

Viré-Clessé, Vieilles Vignes

10 ha; 80,000 bottles

Aurélien Bonhomme's great grandfather planted 4 ha, and his grandfather was the first to bottle his own wine locally. Since 2001, Aurélian and his parents have run the domain, which presently consists of 35 different parcels in Clessé and Viré. Chickens run around the elegant courtyard. The house is at one side, with a rather striking aviary outside the winery, which is partly under reconstruction; at the other side is a workmanlike warehouse, built three years ago, small but with everything packed in. There's a couple of hectares behind the house, with the remaining vineyards scattered around the hills of Viré and Clessé.

Estate production is expanded by purchases of grapes harvested with their own pickers; "80,000 bottles would be a large number for 10 ha!", Aurélian says. All the wines are Viré-Clessé except for a little Mâcon Villages (sold in the U.S.) and some Crémant de Bourgogne. The classic part of production is about five wines. Style varies across the range. Les Pierres Blanches (vinified in stainless steel) and Les Brenillons (vinified in foudres) are intended for relatively early consumption, within five to seven years. Cuvée Spéciale (the major part of production) is a blend using both stainless steel and (old) oak; and Vieilles Vignes increases oak usage to 70%, with less than 20% new oak. These are intended to age for fifteen years or so. Where oak is used, "We are moving from barriques to 400 liter casks to get more harmony," Aurélian explains.

Domaine Ferret ★★

61 rue du Plan, 71960 Fuissé

(33) 03 85 35 61 56

abraccini@domaine-ferret.com

Audrey Braccini

www.domaine-ferret.com

Pouilly-Fuissé

Pouilly-Fuissé, Le Clos

19 ha; 80,000 bottles

Now part of Jadot's expansion into southern Burgundy, Domaine Ferret started as a family business in 1840. In the present era, Mme. Jeanne Ferret, who took over after 1974 when her husband died, was one of the first to focus on single vineyards. There was some modernization when her daughter, Colette, took over in 1993. In 2006, when Colette died, there was no family to inherit; Jadot had been buying must from Ferret for fifty years, and bought the estate in 2008.

There is a lovely courtyard with the old winery just close to the church, and the vineyards of Le Clos and Les Perrières are on the slope right behind, but wine is now made in a new gravity-feed cellar built a few hundred meters away. The old cellar had the capacity only to vinify 10 ha worth of grapes, because Mme. Ferret sold the rest, but now all the grapes are vinified in the new cellar.

Mme. Ferret divided the wines into three groups: communal, Tête de Cru, and Hors Classe. In the communal wines, Autour de Fuissé comes from around Fuissé, and Sous Vergisson comes from Vergisson. As Tête de Crus there are Le Clos, Clos de Prouges, and Les Perrières; and as Hors Classe there are Les Ménétrières and Tournant de Pouilly. Mme. Ferret used to prefer the fuller weight of wines from Fuissé rather than the more delicate wines of Vergisson, and usually harvested late to increase power. Since Audrey Braccini took over as winemaker for Jadot, harvesting has moved earlier, and the style has lightened.

Château-Fuissé ★★

Le Plan, 71960 Fuissé

(33) 03 85 35 61 44

domaine@chateau-fuisse.fr

Antoine Vincent

www.chateau-fuisse.fr

Pouilly-Fuissé

Pouilly-Fuissé, Le Clos

36 ha; 150,000 bottles

This is one of the most important producers in Pouilly Fuissé, with wines representing the classic character of the appellation. The Vincent family have been making wine here since 1862: Antoine Vincent, who took over from his father in 2003, is the fifth generation. There are more than a hundred vineyard plots, mostly in Fuissé with some in Pouilly. Holdings have changed little since the addition of Les Combettes twenty years ago. Soils are heterogeneous. "Even in Les Clos, which is 2.5 ha based on limestone soil just behind the winery, there are differences from top to bottom, so the top is vinified in 1- or 2-year-old barriques to respect the minerality, but at the bottom we can use more new oak," Antoine says. Vinification varies with the vintage: malolactic fermentation depends on the acid balance, and some vintages have extensive battonage while others have little.

About 20 lots are vinified individually; the single vineyards remain separate, but others are blended. There are two cuvées at Pouilly-Fuissé village level, Tête de Cuvée and Vieilles Vignes (from 50- to 80-year-old vines in nine plots planted by Antoine's grandfather). There are three single vineyard bottlings, Les Brûlées (relatively powerful), Les Combettes (relatively delicate), and Le Clos (one of the top cuvées of the appellation). The overall style is firm and full-flavored.

In addition to Pouilly-Fuissé, there's some St. Véran and Mâcon, and most recently some Juliénas from Beaujolais (Domaine De La Conseillère). There's also a negociant business under the Vincent label that gives an aperçu into the house style at a lower price level, including Mâcon Villages and St. Véran as well as the Marie Antoinette Pouilly Fuissé.

Domaine des Vignes du Maynes   *

⟳ *Sagy, 71260 Cruzille*

📞 *(33) 03 85 33 20 15*

@ *info@vignes-du-maynes.com*

▣ *Julien Guillot*

🌐 *www.vignes-du-maynes.com*

◉ *Mâcon*

🍾 *Beaujolais-Leynes*

🍾 *Bourgogne Rouge, Auguste*

🔲❗ 🍇

◖ *7 ha; 30,000 bottles*

Located North of Mâcon, but producing wine from both Mâcon and Beaujolais, the domain produces reds from both Gamay and Pinot Noir as well as its white Mâcon. They are proud of the history: vines were first planted here by the monks of Cluny in 910, and pressing takes place on wooden wine presses dating from 1895. The Guillots have owned the estate since 1954, and it is now in the hands of the third generation.

All red wines are made in the same way; the Guillots are followers of Jules Chauvet, and use semi-carbonic maceration; intact berries have ten days of carbonic maceration, and then fermentation is completed conventionally. All wines (red and white) rest on the lees in barriques for eleven months. Wines come mostly from the estate, which consists of a single contiguous holding, but are supplemented by a couple of cuvées using grapes purchased from local growers.

The Bourgogne Rouge comes from Pinot Noir, but the red wines from Mâcon, like the Beaujolais, come from Gamay. In spite of the difference in grape variety, the same style runs through all red cuvées, with fruits showing purity and precision. You might say that the Guillots are making Burgundian wines in Beaujolais.

Domaine Héritiers du Comte Lafon   *

71960 Milly-Lamartine

(33) 03 85 37 78 09

heritiers.lafon@wanadoo.fr

Caroline Gon

www.comtes-lafon.fr

Mâcon

Mâcon-Milly-Lamartine

21 ha; 140,000 bottles

This is not, as its name might suggest, an old domain inherited in the Comte Lafon family, which for several generations has run a top domain in Meursault. In fact, it was an existing domain in Milly Lamartine that Dominique Lafon purchased and renamed in 1999, when he was the first producer from the Côte d'Or to expand into Mâcon. Further vineyards in Uchizy were added in 2003. The latest addition to the range in 2009 was Viré-Clessé, coming from the vineyards of Château de Viré.

Today the vineyard holdings are divided into three roughly equal parts in Milly-Lamartine, Chardonnay-Uchizy, and Viré-Clessé, so that now the domain produces Mâcon, Mâcon-Villages, Mâcon-Milly-Lamartine, and Viré Clessé, together with five single vineyard wines. Production is typically Mâconnais, with the basic wines aged in stainless steel, and some large wood containers used at the upper end.

Dominique describes his objectives as, "I'm not going down to Mâcon to make little Meursault. I'm going to make great Mâcon." The wines are perhaps a little richer than typical for the region, but retain subregional character with the Viré-Clessé, for example, more powerful than the Mâcons. The top wine is the Clos de la Crochette in Mâcon-Chardonnay, a 2.6 ha vineyard originally planted by monks at the Abbey of Cluny. Prices are around a tenth of Lafon's more famous wines from Meursault, but comparisons would be foolish.

Domaine Saumaize-Michelin   **

51 Impasse du Puits, Le Martelet

(33) 03 85 35 84 05

saumaize-michelin@wanadoo.fr

Roger et Christine Saumaize

saumaize-michelin.com

Pouilly-Fuissé

St. Véran, Les Creches

Pouilly-Fuissé, Vignes Blanches

10 ha; 70,000 bottles

The Saumaizes have been making wines for generations in Vergisson, but the domain was formally created when Roger Saumaize married Christine Michelin in 1981. Roger received 4 ha of the family vineyards from his father. (His brother also has a domain under the name of Jacques and Nathalie Saumaize.) "We started mostly with renting vineyards," Christine explains, "slowly the domain grew and we bought vineyards."

A track on the north edge of the village leads up to the domain. Opposite the family house, an old grange was converted into a winery in 1991 and renovated in 2016. "This is Roger's kingdom," Christine says, as we make our way into a vast underground area. "Vergisson is one of the sites of France, so you can only build down, not up," she explains. The cave is stuffed with barriques: all the cuvées are aged in wood, with up to 15% new oak. We tasted at a table outside, under an old vine—"it's 14° in the cave." Walk out into the vineyard behind the house, and you are right under the great Rock of Vergisson.

"The vineyards are all around the rock of Vergisson. This gives our wine a strong minerality," Christine says. The vineyards extend into three appellations, with 15 cuvées coming from Mâcon, St. Véran, and Pouilly-Fuissé (all white except for a Mâcon Rouge). The wines are very fine for their appellations. Mâcon Villages opens with obvious fruits, the impression becomes more elegant and precise moving to St. Véran, and then more concentrated for Les Creches, a single vineyard wine from a very calcareous location just southwest of the rock of Vergisson. There's an increasing sense of minerality with some herbal impressions moving towards Pouilly Fuissé.

The domain made its first cuvée from an individual parcel in 1985, but now there are many cuvées from different lieu-dits in Pouilly Fuissé, the distinction being exposure and how calcareous the soil is. Tasting here is an exercise in terroir. Pentacrine comes from the south side of Vergisson, and is named after a fossil that is common in Vergisson; it's aged in 500 liter barrels "to maintain minerality." Coming from north of the rock, Les Courtelongs is fuller-bodied and tends more towards stone fruits. Vignes Blanches is precise, Les Ronchevats is rounder, La Maréchaude comes from a really steep parcel with ferrous rocks—"so steep no machine can go up, you have to use walking sticks"—and is the most saline. "Clos Sous La Roche is a only a few meters away, but there is a complete change of terroir," with white rocks, making the wine very tense and mineral; this is the most subtle of the cuvées. Most cuvées have 10 months élevage, but Ampelopsis has 20 months, and combines the fullness of Courtelongs with the minerality of the Vergisson cuvées. "It's a selection of fûts that particularly please us from all the climats," Christine says.

The wines make an airy impression with increasing complexity going up the range, as direct fruits become less obvious, while herbal and mineral impressions increase, with a sense of tension and salinity showing in Pouilly Fuissé.

Domaine La Soufrandière   *

125 rue aux Bourgeois, 71680 Vinzelles

(33) 03 85 35 67 72

contact@bretbrothers.com

Jean-Philippe & Jean-Guillaume Brett

www.bretbrothers.com

Pouilly-Vinzelles

Pouilly-Vinzelles, Les Quarts

6 ha; 30,000 bottles

Only a single hectare at the time, the estate was purchased by the Bret family in 1947, but until the late 1990s, grapes were sold to the cooperative. Today the domain is run by three brothers, who produced their first vintage from La Soufrandière in 2000; they created the negociant business of Bret Brothers in 2001. Overall production is divided equally between estate and negociant activity. A modern cave was built in 2000, and doubled in size in 2011.

Each wine for Bret Brothers comes from a single grower (harvested by Soufrandière's pickers); specializing in micro-cuvées (from 900 to 4,000 bottles), they make about 18 bottlings. Estate vineyards are around the property, which looks out over the Saône Valley from just behind the Vinzelles village at 225m elevation. The 4 ha of Pouilly Vinzelles (Les Quartz) are just behind the house, immediately to the west is the small plot of Les Longeays, and there's a hectare of Mâcon Vinzelles coming from the bottom of the slope, below Pouilly Vinzelles.

Wines are aged for a year in barriques: "All barrels are old, 5-15 years, we don't want any new oak," says Jean-Philippe Bret. The estate wines become increasingly subtle going up the hierarchy. Mâcon-Vinzelles is overtly fruity, Pouilly-Vinzelles shows more restraint and adds some citrus, Les Longeays shows more variety and restraint, and Les Quarts becomes hard to place between stone and citrus fruits. The Bret Brothers wines, which cover a wider range, are a little less intense.

Domaine Jean Thévenet

*

Quintaine, 71260 Clessé

(33) 03 85 36 94 03

contact@bongran.com

Jean Thevenet

www.bongran.com

Viré-Clessé

Mâcon, Cuvée Tradition

27 ha; 60,000 bottles

Headquarters for the three domains under Jean Thévenet (not to be confused with Jean-Paul Thévenet in Beaujolais or Jean-Claude Thévenet at Pierreclos) is a modern utilitarian warehouse in Clessé. There is the unusual policy here of dividing the vineyards according to terroirs into domains, so each domain represents one terroir (defined by the proportion of clay to calcareous soil). All are in Viré-Clessé.

Domaine de la Bongran, the largest and best known, was the first of the domains, started two generations back, and then expanded by Jean Thévenet, who was one of the first to introduce organic methods in the region. Domaine Emilian Gillet (the original family name) was founded in 1988 with vines that had been rented. And the smallest, Domaine de Roally, was purchased when its owner retired in 2000 by Gauthier Thévenet, Jean's son.

All three domains are worked in similar ways, but with differences resulting from their characters: fermentation is slower, and élevage is longer for Domaine de la Bongran, so its wines are released later than the others. The wine from Domaine de la Bongran has an exotic quality, the fruits are pushed to the limits of ripeness, and there's a distinct impression of sweetness (the 2006 had 5.5 g/l residual sugar). Perhaps this is the terroir of ripeness. "Wines from this terroir always have residual sugar. But if it's balanced, you don't feel it," says Jean Thévenet. Sometimes there's even a late harvest, botrytized wine.

Domaine Thibert Père et Fils   *

Rue Adrien Arcelin, 71960 Fuisse

(33) 06 75 46 53 98

info@domaine-thibert.com

Sandrine Thibert-Needham

www.domaine-thibert.com

Pouilly-Fuissé

Pouilly-Fuissé

22 ha; 160,000 bottles

"We are a family domain, my parents come from seven generations of vignerons in Fuissé," says Christophe Thibert. "My parents didn't bottle, everything was sold in barrels, today we bottle everything. My grandfather had 12 children, and each constructed his own domain. We set up here in 1967." The domain lies behind an unassuming entrance in the main street next to the village square. Behind is a vast courtyard with winery buildings all around, constructed successively, most recently in 2005 and 2014. There's a spacious tasting room at the front. It has increased several times in size since 1967.

Aside from the communal Bourgogne, the rosé, and the Crémant, there are 13 cuvées from Mâcon Villages, St. Véran, Pouilly Loché, Pouilly Vinzelles, and Pouilly Fuissé. Vinification follows traditional lines, with Mâcon Verze aged in 20% old barriques and 80% stainless steel, St. Véran aged in barriques with a maximum of 10% new oak, and a little more new oak used for the cuvées from the Pouillys. "I want to produce wines where I can smell the fruit, the terroir and the minerality, so I am careful with new oak."

Fruits increase in citric intensity going up the range, Macon Verzé is faintly herbal, the St. Véran cuvées have a little more bite, and Pouilly Loché has more forceful fruits in the same citrus spectrum. Pouilly Fuissé is smoother, starting with the Cuvée Traditionelle. The Vieilles Vignes, from vines that are almost 80 years old, has a stony impression with more weight. Moving in the direction of minerality, the single parcel wines Vignes Blanches and Menétrières are the top of the line, and are worth looking out for.

Maison Verget

***

Sologny, 71960 Sologny

(33) 03 85 51 66 00

contact@verget-sa.com

Jean-Marie Guffens

www.verget-sa.fr

Mâcon

Chablis, Montée de Tonnerre

Pouilly-Fuissé, La Roche

0 ha; 360,000 bottles

"In a good year we make about 55 different wines at Verget. Most of the wines are based on grapes from several growers although for Côte d'Or it may be from a single grower because quantities are small," explains Jean-Marie Guffens. "The philosophy is to make wine that is as good as possible within very complicated rules of the region. Taking in mind that we always prefer precision—we try to make the wines as pure as possible." Verget buys only grapes or must, with the range of cuvées changing from year to year. All wines stay in wood for 8 months and in concrete for 8 months. "You see terroir more clearly if you treat all wines the same," Jean-Marie says.

Created in 1990, Verget is now part of a trilogy of holdings, also including the Guffens-Heynen domain in Mâcon (established in 1979), and Château des Tourettes (purchased in 1997 in the Lubéron). Verget's range includes southern Burgundy (Mâcon, St. Véran, and many cuvées from Pouilly-Fuissé), Chablis (from village wines to Grand Cru), and the Côte d'Or. Verget demonstrates Jean-Marie's view of the potential of an appellation rather than others' historic view of it, with flavorful Pouilly-Fuissé and ripe, intense, Chablis.

The wines from the Guffens-Heynen domain really show what can be done in the region. They have a flavor interest and complexity and texture that in a blind tasting might well be taken for a higher level appellation; in fact it is that deep texture, reminiscent of the Côte d'Or, that for me is Verget's trademark.

Beaujolais

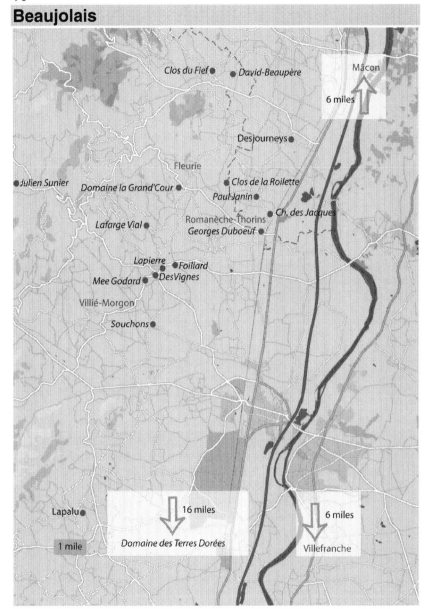

Clos du Fief ● ● David-Beaupère

Mâcon

6 miles

Desjourneys ●

Fleurie

● Julien Sunier

Domaine la Grand'Cour ● ● Clos de la Roilette

Paul Janin ●

Ch. des Jacques

Romanèche-Thorins

Lafarge Vial ● Georges Duboeuf ●

Lapierre ● ● Foillard

● Des Vignes

Mee Godard ●

Villié-Morgon

Souchons ●

Lapalu ●

16 miles

1 mile

Domaine des Terres Dorées

6 miles

Villefranche

Domaine David-Beaupère *

La Bottière 69840, Juliénas

(33) 09 75 92 61 19

louisclement.david@gmail.com

Louis-Clement David-Beaupere

www.domainedavidbeaupere.fr

Juliénas

Juliénas, La Bottière

9 ha; 35,000 bottles

A tasting here is not quite the usual experience. When we arrived, operatic choruses were coming out of the house. We could still hear the opera faintly in the tasting room. Louis-Clément explains that the family runs a music school. His grandfather bought the domain in the 1960s after returning from Algeria where he used to make wine. "My father was a doctor, and the vineyards were rented out. The renter retired in 2004 so I was able to take over 4 ha. I became organic almost straight away, and made my first vintage in 2008. I'm still the only organic producer in Juliénas."

Vineyards are mostly in Juliénas, with a large holding in the La Bottière *climat* near the winery. "In 2015 I took over another 4 ha, so I doubled the area all at once." This was 2 ha in La Vayolette (in Juliénas) and 2 ha in Moulin-à-Vent. "Vinification is semi- to almost full carbonic maceration. There's only one pump-over as the idea is to have carbonic maceration. Juliénas is a strong terroir—it can be rustic—at the beginning I started making wine with a lot of extract, but it means the wines have to be kept a long time, and I wanted to have something more immediate."

The Juliénas is the main cuvée, coming from young vines in La Bottière, but it will become a blend when La Vayolette is certified organic. It's aged only in tank. Silky and aromatic, it's intended for immediate enjoyment. The La Bottière cuvée comes from the oldest vines, around 70 years, with lower yields. It's also aged in tank. "Until 2014 I aged La Bottière in wood, but it's too much for the wine," Louis-Clément says. Longer maceration gives more presence on the palate, still in the style of carbonic maceration, with lovely aromatics against a silky background. La Vayolette comes from the classic blue rock terroir; a more powerful wine in the same style, it is soft, almost voluptuous. The domain offers an unusual opportunity to see different terroirs represented through the style of carbonic maceration.

Domaine du Clos du Fief   *

Les Gonnands, 69840 Juliénas

(33) 04 74 04 41 62

domaine@micheltete.com

Michel Tete

www.micheltete.com

Juliénas

Juliénas, Cuvée Prestige

14 ha; 80,000 bottles

"It's been a family domain for four generations," says Françoise Tête. "When my husband, Michel, took over, it was only 6 ha. Michel expanded the domain, and since 2015, Sylvain has been working with his father, and he has added two new appellations, Chénas and Moulin-à-Vent." The label has changed from Michel Tête to Sylvain & Michel Tête.

The main focus is on local vineyards in Juliénas, which represent about half the domain. Most of the other half is Beaujolais Villages, which produces red, rosé, and white. The time that Michel Tête spent in Burgundy shows in his approach to winemaking, which ranges from traditional semi-carbonic maceration to completely Burgundian, depending on the cuvée.

Beaujolais Villages comes from close to Juliénas, on friable rocky soil. Made by semi-carbonic maceration, this is very much a modern Beaujolais, light, fruity, and tart. St. Amour gets a mixed approach, mostly semi-carbonic, but with 20% destemmed: it's rounder and softer than Beaujolais Villages, but follows the traditional Beaujolais style.

For Juliénas, there are three cuvées. Cuvée Tradition is all whole bunch (semi-carbonic) vinification in cement, and is aged entirely in cement; it's soft and approachable, with more presence than the St. Amour. Cuvée Prestige comes from three plots of old vines, aged from 80 to 100 years, with very small yields; aged half in cement and half in old tonneaux, there's more sense of structure, although still showing that soft, approachable, house style. Tête de Cuvée comes from a single parcel on terroir of blue rocks. It's 100% destemmed—"this is not the Beaujolais method, it's the Burgundian method," says Sylvain—and is vinified in a wooden cuve and then aged in tonneau of old wood. It shows more structure against that characteristic soft background. Very approachable for Juliénas, the wines are ready to drink on release.

Domaine Jules Desjourneys ★★

📍 *75 rue Jean Thorin Pontanevaux, 71570 La Chapelle de Guinchay*

📞 *33 (0)3 85 23 11 10*

@ *contact@julesdesjourneys.fr*

👤 *Fabien Duperray*

🌐 *www.julesdesjourneys.fr*

⚫ *Moulin-à-Vent*

🍾 *Fleurie, La Chapelle des Bois*

🚫 ⚟ 🍇

🍇 *7 ha; 20,000 bottles*

Fabien Duperray started as a distributor, but when he acquired some very old vines in the Beaujolais crus in 2007, he switched to becoming a producer. "One day I was offered a parcel of Les Moriers that was as steep as Côte Rôtie and I couldn't resist—now it's my passion," Fabien says. Since then he has added other plots, and now produces several single vineyard cuvées, mostly from Fleurie and Moulin à Vent, as well as appellation wines. His vineyards are on the steepest slopes of the appellations, and are worked manually. Like any producer bringing quality to a region in difficulties, he has had problems with the authorities, and the 2008 l'Interdit is from Fleurie but labeled Vin de France because it was refused the agrément to be labeled as an AOP wine.

There's no fixed mindset here: some years Fabien is the first to pick, some years the last. Winemaking is traditional, with whole clusters fermented for a month, malolactic fermentation delayed by a cooling system, and the wines matured for 18 months in barrique. Production averages a few hundred cases for each of the single vineyard cuvées. The web site identifies the location of the domain as "Bourgogne de Sud," but although the wines are often compared to the Côte de Nuits, they are not Beaujolais pretending to be Burgundy, but very much their own maximal expression of Gamay. Helped no doubt by low yields from the old vines (some over 100-years-old), the sheer intensity of the fruits brings out Gamay's slightly higher-toned aromatics. Higher alcohol than usual for Beaujolais is a natural part of the style.

None of these are wines for instant gratification; all are serious wines requiring some aging. The typicity of each appellation really comes out, showing generosity for Fleurie and more reserve for Moulin à Vent. Single vineyard wines are more finely structured than the appellation wines; in fact the main difference is not the flavor spectrum but the level of refinement.

Domaine Louis et Claude Desvignes ★

135 rue de La Voute, 69910 Villié Morgon

(33) 04 74 04 23 35

louis.desvignes@wanadoo.fr

Louis & Claude Desvignes

www.louis-claude-desvignes.com

Morgon

Morgon, Côte de Py

11 ha; 50,000 bottles

Devoted exclusively to Morgon, the domain is built around a courtyard just off one of the oldest streets in the village of Villié-Morgon. "We are at least the eighth generation, perhaps more because records were lost in the Revolution," says Louis-Benoît Desvignes. We had our tasting in an old cave. "This is the barrel cellar, but we don't use any barrels in my family, we think cement tanks are more interesting for what we are looking for. We have a lot of interesting flavors in the soils of Morgon, we want to preserve them. The wine is left alone in tank for 10 months or more with no racking until bottling," Louis-Benoît explains.

Depending on the vintage, there may be four or five cuvées, including the Côte du Py, where the Desvignes have 5 ha, half on the top of the hill and the rest in parcels lower down. A Vieilles Vignes cuvée comes from two small parcels of hundred-year-old vines on the hill. House style shows a linear purity to the fruits; some people might be inclined to call this minerality. The cuvées reflect their terroirs. The Vieilles Vignes has concentration as well as purity, and I might be inclined to place it in Moulin-à-Vent in a blind tasting or perhaps to think about Pommard. The Javernières, from a parcel in Côte du Py, has a softer impression than the Côte du Py itself: "They used to say 'Pinoté' to mean that some wines have a Burgundian character, and this is a very good example," says Louis-Benoît. Indeed, the subtlety of the cuvées is reminiscent of a tasting in Burgundy.

Georges Duboeuf *

Hameau Duboeuf, 71570 Romanèche-Thorins

(33) 03 85 35 34 20

conso@duboeuf.com

Franck Duboeuf

www.duboeuf.com

Beaujolais

Fleurie, Rein de Gré

0 ha; 22,000,000 bottles

Duboeuf's headquarters at Romanèche-Thorins, on the eastern edge of the Beaujolais near Moulin-à-Vent, represent a vast enterprise, signposted as Hameau Duboeuf, with a museum, tasting room, bookshop, and all the facilities you could want. Hameau Duboeuf makes it sound smaller than it really is: there are villages in the Beaujolais that are smaller than this. Signifying the discrepancy between Duboeuf and other producers, the vast winery occupies more than 6 ha—around the size of the average producer in Beaujolais.

Duboeuf produces Gamay everywhere it is grown in France, including Beaujolais, Mâconnais, Pays d'Oc, Côtes du Rhône, Ardèche, and Touraine. Famous for his tasting ability, Georges still tastes every wine that is bottled. "I spend two hours tasting every day," he says. The vast range extends from Nouveau, through Beaujolais and Beaujolais Villages, to the Crus. The Flower series is the best known, but there is an increasing number of individual cuvées indicated by the origin of the grower.

The model remains as it started, as a negociant buying grapes (for whites the grower presses the grapes and Duboeuf takes the must). The top line, Cuvée Prestige, is an assemblage of the best lots, depending on the year, but is available only in France. The house style (insofar as a style can be defined for such a wide range) is for open, forward fruits, giving a fresh impression on the palate with supple tannins in the background. The Fleurie is perhaps the epitome of this style.

Domaine Jean Foillard

Le Clachet, Villié Morgon, 69910

(33) 04 74 04 24 97

jean.foillard@wanadoo.fr

Jean Foillard

Morgon

Morgon, Côte du Py

16 ha; 100,000 bottles

One of the founder members of the "gang of four" who modernized Beaujolais, Jean Foillard took over his father's domain in 1980. The winery is an old farm that Jean and Agnes Foillard renovated, on the main road out of Villié-Morgon, close to the Côte du Py; it now also offers bed and breakfast for visitors.

Most of the vineyards are in Morgon, with the largest holding on Côte du Py; there's also a vineyard in the lieu-dit Corcelette in the north of Morgon that was inherited from Agnes's parents. There are smaller holdings in Fleurie, and just outside Morgon in Beaujolais (the source for the Beaujolais Nouveau). Winemaking is the same for all cuvées, using semi-carbonic maceration with no added sulfur.

There are six cuvées altogether, with three from Morgon. The Morgons are distinguished by terroir and vine age: the Morgon Classique is an assemblage, and is the only wine not to be matured in wood; cuvée Corcelette, the lightest of the single vineyard wines, comes from 80-year-old vines on sandstone, and is matured in foudres; Côte du Py, by far Foillard's best known cuvée, comes from vines of varying age on schist and granite, and is matured in barriques; and cuvée 3.14 (which carries a jazzy pi sign on the label, and has been made since 2003 only in the best vintages) comes from 100-year-old vines on the Côte du Py. Foillard's wines have a lightness of touch that has often led to comparisons with Chambolle Musigny, with the Morgan single vineyard wines showing classic tension.

Domaine Mee Godard   *

◎ *Morgan le Bas, 69910 Villié Morgon*

📞 *+33 06 66 47 00 64*

@ *domaine.meegodard@yahoo.fr*

▣ *Mee Godard*

🌐 *www.meegodard.com*

◉ *Morgon*

🍾 *Morgon, Grand Cras*

🚜 *6 ha; 25,000 bottles*

Mee Godard was studying biology at university when her father suggested she might become an oenologist, and a minor in wine science led her to Oregon and then back to France. Why Beaujolais? "Because I discovered these wines at a tasting in the region. When I left my winemaking job in Beaune, I came here to look for vineyards." At the end of 2012 she was able to buy in house in Morgon that came with 5 ha of vineyards. A year later she was about to add another hectare in Moulin à Vent, and in 2017 another hectare. The average age of vines in the domain is 60-65 years (a 1 ha plot has 20-year-old vines). The house is just at the edge of Côte du Py. The domain is a work in progress, with the house slowly being renovated.

Mee's winemaking is distinctive. "I try to make vins de garde. I try to use as much whole bunch as possible, mostly about 70%, so there is some carbonic maceration, but I don't want to have a lot, just some in individual berries." Both punch-down and pumping-over are used. Everything is aged in wood, using a mixture of barriques, demi-muids, and foudres with only a little new wood. "Last year I didn't buy any new wood, the year before I bought a new demi-muid."

These are certainly wines for aging, quite reserved at first with a distinct tannic presence. They can be tight and austere with a touch of menthol turning medicinal in cooler vintages. There is certainly an impression of lots of extraction. Even rich vintages like 2015 give a strong sense of structure. The alcohol can be as high as 14% or more.

The 5 ha of Morgon are in three different climats, and each makes a separate cuvée. Corcelette tends to show red berry fruits with a touch of tannin at the end, Grand Cras is a little broader with just a touch more aromatic lift, and Côte du Py is the roundest and richest, but always with that sense of tension and precision waiting to emerge. There is also a barrel selection from a 1 ha plot in Côte du Py, called Passerelle 557, which shows great purity of fruits. Fruits move from red towards black along the series. These are real wines expressing terroir but they need time to develop, at least two or three years after release; they prompt a comparison with Burgundy.

Domaine de la Grand'Cour   *

La Grand'Cour 69820, Fleurie

(33) 04 74 69 84 16

jlouis.dutraive@orange.fr

Jean-Louis Dutraive

dutraive.jeanlouis.free.fr

Brouilly

Fleurie, Clos de la Grand'Cour

11 ha; 40,000 bottles

"My great grandfather bought our first vines, and we've been vignerons father to son for five generations," says Jean-Louis Dutraive. "We weren't in Fleurie at first, my father bought this domain in 1969." The winery is in the middle of the *clos* of Grand'Cour, which represents about half of the estate vineyards. A house is on one side of the courtyard, with winery buildings on the other side. There are vast cellars underneath. "At one point the domain was 20 ha and the facilities match, but my father only bought part of the vineyards," Jean-Louis explains. There are two labels. Domaine de la Grand'Cour is used for estate grapes. Jean Louis Dutraive is used to label wine made from purchased grapes.

"Vinification starts by putting grapes in a cold chamber at 6-7.5°C. Then we do nothing, not even temperature control. We don't want to extract too much, that's why we start at low temperature. The yeast are efficient even then, and temperatures don't go over 18°. We use barriques but usually some aging is done in stainless steel to maintain freshness." The mix varies with the cuvée, from equal proportions of all barriques, foudres, and stainless steel for the wine from the *clos,* to 100% barriques for the Vieilles Vignes.

Most of the vineyards are in large blocks close to the domain, and there are separate cuvées for each terroir. Two cuvées come from the Grand'Cour monopole surrounding the house: the Clos de la Grand'Cour, and the Vielles Vignes, from vines about 70 years old. Outside of the Grand'Cour there are two terroirs in Fleurie, Champagne (immediately south of Grand'Cour) and Chapelle des Bois (the other side of the road). Because hail reduced the crop greatly in 2016, there was a Tous Ensemble bottling of Vieilles Vignes blended from all the holdings in Fleurie (it is very good).

The style of the Fleurie cuvées is fresh, emphasizing red fruits, elegant rather than fleshy, and is similar for the Jean-Louis Dutraive wines and the Grand'Cour estate, but Grand'Cour wines show more intensity. The Vieilles Vignes cuvée of Brouilly (from 50-year-old vines) is in the same style, perhaps a touch more four-square.

Château des Jacques ★★★

Les Jacques, 71570 Romanèche Thorins

(33) 03 85 35 51 64

chateau-des-jacques@wanadoo.fr

Cyril Chirouze

www.chateau-des-jacques.fr

Moulin-à-Vent

Moulin-à-Vent, Clos du Grand Carquelin

88 ha; 350,000 bottles

For years, Château des Jacques, under the ownership of the Thorin family, produced a single wine that was the best in Moulin-à-Vent, quite Burgundian in its capacity to develop with age. The estate was purchased by Burgundian negociant Louis Jadot in 1996, and then in 2001 Jadot extended the range by adding the Bellevue estate in Morgon, more or less doubling the size of the domain. There are 37 ha in Moulin-à-Vent, and 28 ha in Morgon. The wines are vinified following Burgundian practice (destemming and avoiding carbonic maceration) and spend several months maturing in barriques. A 9 ha plot of Chardonnay has also been added, producing both Bourgogne Blanc and Beaujolais Blanc.

Château des Jacques occupies an extensive park on the outskirts of Romanèche Thorins; major renovations in 2017 turned it into a building site, when a new cuverie was constructed, and the existing buildings completely renovated. The new cuverie is only for winemaking; the wine will continue to be aged in the seventeenth century cellars underneath. "The idea is not to change the style, but to be able to make the wine more precise," says winemaker Cyril Chirouze. The cuverie has a mixture of stainless steel and concrete tanks. "Stainless steel tanks are used with pump-over when the berries are concentrated, but if we think more extraction is needed, we'll use the concrete tanks with punch-down."

"The heart of our philosophy is to produce Gamay reflecting terroir like Pinot Noir does," Cyril explains. "We have two levels of wine: the blends, which I could compare with village wine in Burgundy; and then the single vineyards, which we could compare to premier crus." There is one blend each from Morgon, Fleurie, and Moulin-à-Vent. "Depending on the vintage we produce 7 different single vineyard wines, 6 from Moulin-à-Vent and 1 from Morgon. You might think it is grand vin and second wine philosophy, but it is not at all that; we take the best barrels for the blends, and then if there is enough left over, we make the single vineyard wines."

The Burgundian style means that the wines have enough structure to require some time. The blends all have the same élevage, with one third in tank and two thirds in barrique, with not much new oak. This showcases the differences in terroir, a bit angular, uptight, and reserved for Morgon, fleshier for Fleurie, and broader with more sense of structure for Moulin-à-Vent. All of the single vineyard wines have 20% new oak. The Moulin-à-Vent cuvées show greater fruit concentration than the blends, with that sense of minerality you might describe as iron in the soil. Clos du Grand Carquelin may be the best representation of Gamay, showing the smooth, aromatic character that represents what happens when Gamay is treated as a serious variety. "Carquelin is only 50m from La Roche, but you will see it's different. It is probably one of the poorest soils you can find in France." Carquelin is a little rounder than La Roche, which comes from just below the windmill, and I really like for its more Burgundian character—it might be placed in Pommard in a blind tasting. Clos de Rochegrès has a sense of purity and minerality enhanced by its elevation at 361m; moving to Morgon, Côte du Py at almost the same elevation shows great sense of fruit purity and finesse. The wines drink well from about five years after the vintage to more than ten, and are a benchmark for the Burgundian style in Beaujolais.

Domaine Paul Janin et Fils ★★

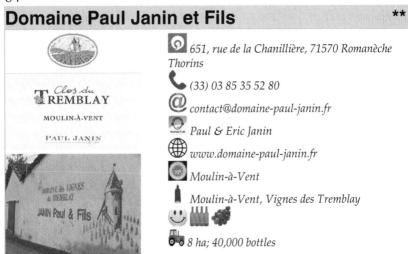

📍 *651, rue de la Chanillière, 71570 Romanèche Thorins*

📞 *(33) 03 85 35 52 80*

@ *contact@domaine-paul-janin.fr*

Paul & Eric Janin

🌐 *www.domaine-paul-janin.fr*

Moulin-à-Vent

Moulin-à-Vent, Vignes des Tremblay

🙂 🏭 🌿

🚜 *8 ha; 40,000 bottles*

"The history is very simple. Like many family domains it goes back to my great grandfather, who was a tonnelier and bought several parcels of vines. The domain has both increased and diminished. My grandfather rented some vineyards and bought some in an old lieu-dit, Tremblay, which became the name of the domain. My father rented some more parcels, and he was able to buy some of them later," explains Eric Janin, who came into the domain with his father in 1983, and took over when Paul retired in 2008. (Retired or not, Paul is still quite busy in the tasting room.)

Various labels are used, including Domaine des Vignes des Jumeaux for the Beaujolais Villages, or Domaine des Vignes du Tremblay, but the important thing to look for on the label is Paul Janin. Vinification is traditional, meaning mostly whole clusters for semi-carbonic maceration, with just a little destemming, and aging in stainless steel. Vinification and élevage are basically the same for all cuvées.

The domain is very much focused on Moulin-à-Vent, with just a hectare in Beaujolais Villages (both white and black). The wines are the quintessence of the style of maturation in cuve, emphasizing purity of black fruits, with tannins evident on the finish, but always supple. The Beaujolais Villages is quite restrained for the appellation, fresh and not too aromatic. There are three cuvées of Moulin-à-Vent. Vignes des Tremblay is an assemblage from several plots in the Tremblay lieu-dit (including some very old vines); it has that typical sense of purity and is very stylish. Heritage du Tremblay is an assemblage from plots of old vines, based on plantings by Eric's grandfather in the 1930s, with an average age over 90 years. Produced as a separate cuvée since 1991, this is the flagship of the domain. Les Greneriers is a single vineyard wine, made as a separate cuvée since

2009, and coming from a 1 ha plot planted before 1914 and purchased in 1967, where very low yields give a great sense of purity. (It is matured in demi-muids.) There is greater concentration in the vieilles vignes and single vineyard wines, but always that sense of purity and focus. The style carries over to the whites.

Domaine Jean-Claude Lapalu *

CÔTE DE BROUILLY

Appellation Côte de Brouilly Contrôlée

2010

MIS EN BOUTEILLE À LA PROPRIÉTÉ
JEAN CLAUDE LAPALU
13% vol. — 75 cl
"Le Petit Vernay" — 69460 St. Etienne la Varenne — France
PRODUIT DE FRANCE

Le Fourque, 69460 Saint Étienne La Varenne

(33) 04 74 03 50 57

jean-claudelapalu@wanadoo.fr

Jean Claude Lapalu

Brouilly

Brouilly, Vieilles Vignes

12 ha; 60,000 bottles

Jean-Claude takes Beaujolais to the extremes of late picking and high alcohol. Usually in Beaujolais an elevated alcohol level indicates chaptalization, but here it indicates extreme ripeness. In the 2009 vintage, some of the wines were labeled at 14.5% alcohol. (Levels came back down to 13% in 2011.) Viticulture is biodynamic, and yields are low, usually under 35 hl/ha.

Jean-Claude took over the domain from his father in 1996. Grapes had previously been sold to the cooperative, but Jean-Claude started making wine in 2000. His wines are unusual for Brouilly, which usually isn't particularly well distinguished from Beaujolais Villages, but here there is distinctly more structure.

Aside from the Beaujolais Villages Vieilles Vignes cuvée, the emphasis is on Brouilly and Côte de Brouilly, where there are eight separate parcels of vines. There are wines from each cru, cuvées from Vieilles Vignes, and the Croix de Rameaux from a single parcel near the winery in Brouilly. Altogether there are six cuvées.

Vinification is traditional, but there is reduced use of carbonic maceration for Côte de Brouilly and Croix des Rameaux, which are matured in old barriques. There are experiments with maturing wine in amphorae. Winemaking follows natural precepts, including minimal use of sulfur, but the style makes a very rich impression. Some critics have described the style as "Beaujolais meets Priorat."

Domaine Marcel Lapierre ★★

Rue Rabelais, Villié Morgon, 69910

(33) 04 74 04 23 89

informations@marcel-lapierre.com

Mathieu Lapierre

www.marcel-lapierre.com

Morgon

Morgon

16 ha; 105,000 bottles

The name of Marcel Lapierre became a symbol of the revival of "serious" wine in the Beaujolais. The domain itself existed before the Revolution, but took its modern form after phylloxera under Marcel Lapierre's grandfather. It was among the first in the region to bottle its own wine. Marcel Lapierre initiated the move away from the image of Beaujolais as following semi-industrial techniques for making cheap and cheerful wine.

Located in the town of Villié-Morgon, the domain is divided into two separate sets of buildings; we tasted the wines in a courtyard surrounded by buildings constructed just after the Revolution. Today the domain is run by Mathieu Lapierre, who is continuing his father's focus on natural wine-making. The domain is completely in Morgon, but some of the production from young vines is declassified to Vin de France; "Young Gamay is very productive," explains Mathieu. When the year is sufficiently good there is a Vieilles Vignes bottling; this is the cuvée Marcel Lapierre.

Sulfur is always low, but some cuvées are bottled entirely without any. There's always a difference. "There's no rule, it depends on the vintage whether the wine with or without sulfur has more generosity," Mathieu says. My impression most often is that keeping sulfur down increases expression of fruit purity. Certainly the house style is towards a certain linear purity of fruits, quite tight and precise when young, and needing some time to open out.

Dominique Piron   *

📍 Morgon, 69910 Villié Morgon

📞 (33) 04 74 69 10 20

@ dominiquepiron@domaines-piron.fr

Dominique Piron

🌐 www.domaines-piron.fr

Morgon

🍾 Morgon, Grand Cras

🚜 95 ha; 550,000 bottles

"We go back a long time, four centuries in Morgon," says Dominique Piron, whose domain occupies a group of buildings just below the Côte de Py. How many hectares do you have, I asked. "More and more, we are the principal producer in Beaujolais, mostly in Morgon, but also with a good diversity of other appellations. We have lots of small parcels. We buy some grapes but it's not essential, mostly we use our estate grapes. There are 15 cuvées, including 8 crus, with 4 cuvées in Morgon." Côte du Py was the first *climat* to be made as a separate cuvée, in 1996, and the others have followed. The Morgons all have different colors on the label to symbolize the different soils.

Do you use carbonic maceration? "Well what is that for you? It's really no more than using whole berries. For the crus we destem a large proportion of grapes because we want to bring out terroir. Our vinification is mostly traditional Burgundian with punch-down and pump-over. With Côte du Py or Moulin a Vent, for example, there are almost three weeks of maceration—we are looking for terroir." There is some élevage in wood only for the Morgons, a bit more for Côte du Py than the others.

"I don't know if you can talk of a style for the domain, each terroir is different, but we look for freshness and aromatic complexity, with a good balance. Many of the terroirs are calcareous with clay. When we get to granite, we look for delicacy. We'd rather have a wine that develops some complexity than one you can drink straight away in the modern style. Complexity does not come from vinification but from the soil."

The wines are quite sturdy. Beaujolais Blanc and Villages are light, fruity, and aromatic. Going to the crus, the wines become more serious, and with the cuvées from Morgon, the effects of long maceration are seen as tannic structure on the finish that requires a couple of years to integrate.

Morgon La Chanaise is an assemblage from many plots. Showing that classic taut quality of granite, "it's very representative of the terroir of Morgon," Dominique says. Grand Cras comes from the south of the appellation, and is a little weightier. The top Morgon is, of course, Côte du Py, distinguished not so much by more power but by that typical combination of tautness and smoothness. Piron's top wine is probably the Chénas Quartz, which comes from an unusual parcel of 9 ha in Chénas where the granite is covered by Quartz crystals. It shows more generosity than the Morgon in the same general style.

Domaine Coudert Clos de La Roilette   *

La Roilette, 69820 Fleurie

(33) 04 74 69 84 37

contact@closdelaroilette.com

Alain Coudert

www.clos-de-la-roilette.com

Fleurie

Fleurie

13 ha; 55,000 bottles

The winery is located on a high point with views over the towns of Fleurie and Moulin-à-Vent. A workmanlike group of buildings is surrounded by vineyards; about half of the holdings are in the immediate vicinity, with the rest elsewhere in Fleurie except for 1 ha about 15 km away in Brouilly. Alain Coudert's father bought the domain in 1967, a small part of a 100 ha estate that was being sold. "We have a terroir that is a little different from the rest of the commune; it's granite but it's older and more decomposed. And when you get up to the border with Moulin-à-Vent, the soils have more clay and give more structured wine," Alain explains. (Before the appellations were created, some of the wine had actually been labeled as Moulin-à-Vent.) To get a more typical Fleurie Alain usually includes lots from the other holdings.

There are usually three cuvées of Fleurie: Clos de Roilette is an assemblage, Cuvée Tardive is a Vieilles Vignes, coming from 80-year-old vines close to the winery (tardive indicates that the wine is intended for aging), and Griffe de Marquis comes from the same vines as Cuvée Tardive, but is matured in barriques of 6-year wood for one year. Cuvée Christal, made in some years, is the antithesis of Tardive: made from young vines for early drinking. Vinification is traditional (using semi-carbonic maceration). The house style is relatively sturdy: the wines are firmer than you usually find with Fleurie, and, at least when young, do not have that open fleshiness.

Domaine des Souchons

Morgon, 69910 Villié Morgon

(33) 04 74 69 14 45

contact@1752.fr

Baptiste Condemine

www.domaine-souchons.com

Morgon

Morgon, Cuvée Claude Pillet

14 ha; 80,000 bottles

The domain has been in the family since 1752 and has vineyards in 47 parcels scattered all over the Morgon appellation. The winery is in a functional group of buildings on the main road outside Villié Morgon. They describe the domain as "resolutely Morgon." "We vinify separately and blend at assemblage," says Baptiste Condemine, who started to modernize things when he came into the estate in 2008. "We should have more cuvées, my father did one, I do two, we should have five. We understand all the different *climats* of Morgon." In addition to the estate wines coming from Morgon, a small negociant activity (SARL 1752) extends the range into the other crus as well as Beaujolais and Beaujolais Villages.

In Morgon, the general bottling is Cuvée Lys; this is on the light side (and is extended by a bottling under screwcap called cuvée Tradition that's overtly for current drinking). The second major cuvée is Claude Pillet, which Baptiste introduced in 2009, named for his grandfather. This is a Vieilles Vignes bottling, coming from vines that are more than a hundred years old at Javernières on the Côte du Py. "This is more like Burgundy style," Baptiste says. Vinification starts in concrete for one month, then the wine is pressed off into barrel before fermentation has finished; fermentation is followed by MLF, and then a third is racked off to barriques of new oak, and the rest is matured in cuve. From the 2012 vintage there is a new cuvée, matured entirely in barriques, from the Grand Cras terroir.

Julien Sunier ★★

Ferme des Noisetiers, 69430 Avenas

📞 (33) 04 74 69 91 74

@ contact@julien-sunier.com

Julien Sunier

🌐 www.julien-sunier.com

Morgon

Fleurie

8 ha; 35,000 bottles

"Here we are, 750m high, and there are no vineyards," Julien says. "The vineyards stop at 600m." Well off the beaten track for Beaujolais, Julien has a house and winery in a spectacular setting high up in the hills above Avenas (a few miles northwest of the Beaujolais crus). Originally purchased as somewhere to live when Julien came to Beaujolais, at the end of a long single track leading off from the main road to Avenas, the house is a stylish conversion of an old cow shed, and there is a small practical winery opposite.

"My parents live in Dijon but my family is not in the wine business. I made wine for other people for twenty years, in France and Italy. I came to Beaujolais in 2003 to start a new winery for Mommessin. I came with a bad idea of Beaujolais—the nouveau idea—but I discovered Beaujolais quickly because I had to buy the grapes for several crus, and I decided to start a little domain on my own in 2007. I'm renting vineyards, and I may change them, but I'll settle the domain around the present size."

Winemaking is a mix of the traditional and modern. It starts with carbonic maceration with the grapes covered by a layer of carbon dioxide. Maceration varies. "Depending on the year, I will macerate from 2 days to 35 days. I don't look for extract, I won't do punch-down or pump-over. We have natural coolness because fermentation is outside at 700m. So even when there is long maceration there is not too much extraction. I want the vintage to express itself." The crus are mostly aged in barriques, using only old wood, varying from 10-15 years. "I do not use any young oak. I like to keep the fruit fresh so we don't like to age too long, the average is 8 months, but we won't go over 12 months. When we put the wine in the barrel, it's still fermenting, and because I don't use any sulfur before bottling, it really has the lees." A fraction of each cru is usually matured in cuve to keep freshness. One feature of the style is that alcohol levels are moderate, usually 12.5% or even less.

Because hailstorms seriously reduced the crop two years running, Julien purchased grapes for his entry-level wine, a Vin de France called Wild Soul, which shows slightly spicy red fruits with just a touch of aromatics. It's declassified to Vin de France because of continuous problems getting the agrément for the AOP. "The people who do the agrément don't like my style, they like thermovinification. I'll play the game for the crus, but not for this." But Wild Soul is a real wine, quite a contrast with the high-toned aromatics of much Beaujolais Villages.

There is one cuvée from each of Julien's three crus. "I blend because I have very small plots in each of the three terroirs, and I think I gain complexity by blending." Regnié is smooth and silky, Fleurie is smooth and spicy with hints of Fleurie's fleshiness showing, and Morgon is taut, crisp, and precise. "This is my favorite cuvée," Julien says. Julien points out that when he was at Mommessin he found an old wine list showing that in the 1920s, the crus of Beaujolais priced the same as Chambolle Musigny, and although he doesn't say it, you feel that his aim is get back there.

Domaine des Terres Dorées   *

Lieu dit Bayere, 69380 Charnay

(33) 04 78 47 93 45

contact@jeanpaulbrun.fr

Jean Paul Brun

Beaujolais

Fleurie

47 ha; 300,000 bottles

The domain is located almost at the southern tip of Beaujolais, but the best known wines come from holdings of the crus in the north. Jean-Paul Brun's grandfather created the domain. "It's always been a zone of polyculture here; my father practiced polyculture. I took over the domain with 4 ha and stopped the polyculture and started to plant white varieties, and then in the 1980s I planted Pinot Noir."

Today there are 9 ha of Chardonnay, 1 ha Roussanne, and 2.5 ha Pinot Noir; the rest is Gamay. The Chardonnay can be labeled as Beaujolais Blanc or Bourgogne, the Pinot Noir is Bourgogne AOP, and the Roussanne is a Vin de France. The Gamay includes 17 ha in crus, including Moulin-à-Vent, Fleurie, and Côte de Brouilly. Beaujolais l'Ancien comes from very old vines. The crus are managed by lutte raisonnée but in the south the domain is organic. Vinification is entirely conventional (with no semi-carbonic maceration).

The house style shows serious wines, without any of the false aromatics that can pump up young Beaujolais and make it superficially attractive when young, but which don't really age in an interesting way. Jean-Paul's wines follow the Burgundian model, and even if Gamay mostly doesn't lend itself to making true Vins de Garde, they move in that direction. Jean-Paul has expanded his production into negociant territory: "To satisfy the demand from people looking for 'true Beaujolais'," he says. He also makes some late harvest botrytized wines.

Jura-Savoie

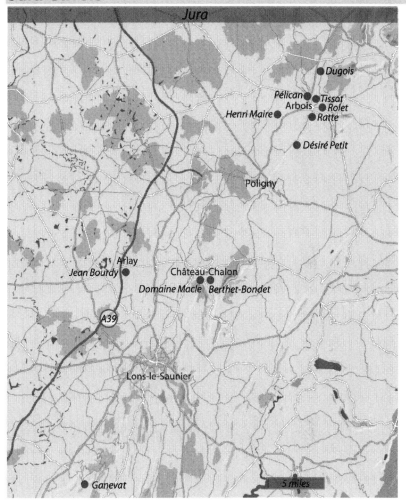

Jura

Dugois

Pélican
Arbois
Henri Maire
Tissot
Rolet
Ratte

Désiré Petit

Poligny

Arlay
Jean Bourdy
Château-Chalon
Domaine Macle   Berthet-Bondet

A39

Lons-le-Saunier

Ganevat

5 miles

Domaine Berthet-Bondet   *

Rue de La Tour, 39210 Château-Chalon

(33) 03 84 44 60 48

berthet-bondet@orange.fr

Jean Berthet Bondet

www.berthet-bondet.net

Château-Chalon

Château-Chalon

11 ha; 40,000 bottles

Jean Berthet-Bondet started the domain in 1985; his family was not previously in wine. "I was attracted by wines and agronomie, I started, I worked abroad, my family had always liked Château-Chalon. The price of vineyards was attractive. People were pulling out vineyards; it was possible to buy." The Berthet-Bondets bought a sixteenth century house with caves underneath, and built a modern winery.

Vineyard holdings are quite broken up, with half in Château-Chalon and half in Côtes de Jura, and more or less equally divided between Chardonnay and Savagnin. There is 1 ha of Poulsard and Trousseau and a tiny parcel of Pinot Noir. The aim is to look for finesse rather than rusticity. Initially there was only wine, under voile in traditional manner, but now there is a Crémant (unusually characterful for the region), a red, and a range of both "classique" (modern) and "tradition" (oxidized under voile) white wines. The type of wine is stated only on the back label, as ouillé or vinifié sur voile.

The classique wines include Chardonnay or Savagnin from the Côtes de Jura; the oxidized wines are an assemblage of Savagnin and Chardonnay from Côtes du Jura (the Tradition cuvée), Savagnin from Côtes de Jura, and Vin Jaune from Château-Chalon. There is also a Vin de Paille and a Macvin. I find the oxidized styles more interesting than the classique, and the best wine by far is the Château-Chalon.

Domaine Jean Bourdy

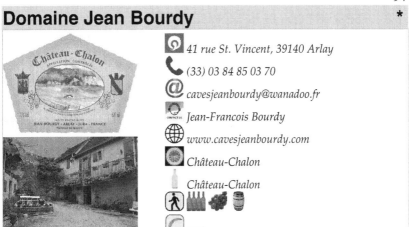

🜚 *41 rue St. Vincent, 39140 Arlay*

📞 *(33) 03 84 85 03 70*

@ *cavesjeanbourdy@wanadoo.fr*

Jean-Francois Bourdy

🌐 *www.cavesjeanbourdy.com*

◉ *Château-Chalon*

🍾 *Château-Chalon*

🚶🏭🍇🛢

🌀 *10 ha*

This is surely one of the most, if not the most, traditional domains in the Jura. Jean-François Bourdy is the fifteenth generation. The house was originally just a kitchen and bedroom, and the sixteenth century caves below are still in use. The vineyards are in Arlay except for some in Château-Chalon. "We have documentation for the production methods for all the old wines, and we follow exactly the same procedures as a hundred years ago; no experimentation or new things," says Jean-François. Bottles have been kept since the eighteenth century, and the library now has 3,000 bottles; vintages for sale go back to the nineteenth century.

How many cuvées do you make, I asked? "We don't make cuvées. We make separate wines: red and white from the Côtes de Jura, Vin Jaune from Château-Chalon, and Vin de Paille, and Macvin, including one made by a (written) recipe from 1579 (which includes spices and herbs). The tradition in the Jura is to have an extended range, but there are no cuvées or vins de cépage."

The tradition at Bourdy is to keep wines for at least four years in old tonneaux before bottling; there are no young wines here. "Never, never, never any new oak: it would be an error because old oak is neutral." The red ("Our village is considered the leader for vin rouge") is traditional to the extent of cofermenting Pinot Noir, Poulsard, and Trousseau; the Côtes de Jura is Chardonnay; the Vin Jaune from Château-Chalon is the most concentrated of all the wines.

Domaine Daniel Dugois *

4 rue de La Mirode, 39600 Les Arsures

(33) 03 84 66 03 41

daniel.dugois@wanadoo.fr

Daniel Dugois

www.vins-danieldugois.com

Arbois

Arbois, Trousseau Grevillière

Arbois, Savagnin Auréoline

10 ha

The domain started when Daniel Dugois bought 2 ha of vineyards and a house in Les Arsures. For the first few years the grapes were sold, and Daniel produced his first vintage in 1982. The domain has been expanded since then, but remains a family business, with Daniel's son, Philippe, joining him in 2003, and taking charge of the vineyards in 2013. White wines include Chardonnay in ouillé style, and Savagnin in both ouillé and sous voile styles, as well as Vin Jaune. There are also several cuvées of Trousseau and a Poulsard. The style here tends to subtlety: nothing is overdone. The Chardonnay is faintly savory, the Savagnin a little more so, with both showing a characteristic smooth texture. The Savagnin sous Voile offers a delicate expression of the oxidative style. The lead red wine is the Trousseau Grevillière, which comes from 60-year-old vines. All the wines are Arbois AOP.

Domaine Ganevat

La Combe, 39190 Rotalier

(33) 03 84 25 02 69

Jean François Ganevat

Côtes de Jura

Côtes de Jura, Grandes Teppes, Chardonnay

10 ha; 40,000 bottles

After working for eight years in Burgundy, Jean-François took over the domain in 1998. Ganevat's cellars run under a row of houses in the main street of a hamlet at the southern tip of the Jura. Extended little by little, the caves are old at one end, but run into a new extension. Vineyards are in many separate parcels. Jean-François has increased the size of the domain a little, and has adopted Burgundian methods for viticulture and vinification. Almost all wines are made in the modern ouillé style, but the occasional oxidized style (such as Cuvée de Pépé) is very fine.

The domain has all five cépages authorized for Côtes de Jura and produces many cuvées from different vineyards, typically around 35 each year. In addition, Jean-François has a reputation for rescuing little known indigenous varieties, which go into Vins de France. He grows 17 grape varieties altogether. The wines offer good expressions of varietal typicity, but I was not blown away by them in the way their reputation would have led me to expect, perhaps because all the wines in an extensive tasting were from barrel: they may just need more time to express themselves. Lees aging is unusually long.

Bottled wines develop a character of minerality and salinity after about four years that is not evident in barrel samples. Those I like best are the Chardonnays from limestone terroirs, which although matured in barriques, resemble unoaked Chablis, at their best perhaps richer and more concentrated. The reds taste sturdier than you would expect from the use of carbonic maceration.

Domaine Henri Maire

 Lieu Dit Boichailles, Arbois, 39600

 (33) 03 84 66 12 34

 client@henri-maire.fr

 www.henri-maire.fr

 Arbois

 300 ha; 3,500,000 bottles

The Maire family had been growing vines in the Jura since the seventeenth century, but it was Henri Maire, who inherited the estate in 1939, who built the domain into the largest in the Jura by purchasing vineyards through the 1950s. The domain accounts for 20% of production in the Jura, and for almost half of the Vin Jaune of Arbois. Henri was a master at marketing, and during the 1950s, the domain became famous for its Vin Fou, bottled in the old style before the completion of fermentation to retain some effervescence in the bottle.

The domain was inherited by his children in 2003, and in 2010 they sold it to an investment group in Luxembourg, who in turn sold it to Boisset of Burgundy at the start of 2015. "We had two problems when we bought it," an informant at Boisset says, "The stocks of old wines and the state of the vineyards." Boisset has started a program to improve the vineyards, and consider that it is now beginning to take effect. It is widely acknowledged that quality had been slipping, but with such extensive holdings there is evidently potential for Maire to become a major force again. Current wines, available in a wide range of styles, are respectable rather than outstanding, and can be found at the tasting room in the center of Arbois.

Domaine Macle

*

Rue de La Roche, 39210 Château-Chalon

(33) 03 84 85 21 85

maclel@wanadoo.fr

Laurent Macle

Château-Chalon

Château-Chalon

12 ha; 40,000 bottles

The Macle family come from barrel makers, and practiced polyculture when they came to Château-Chalon in 1850. In the 1960s they turned exclusively to wine, although the sixteenth century caves make the domain feel much older. Now regarded as one of the oldest producers, the domain has choice vineyard holdings, often on extremely steep slopes. Production here is focused exclusively on white wine; Jean Macle was regarded as one of the most knowledgeable producers of the oxidized style. He was followed by his son Laurent in 1995. The vineyards are divided into 8 ha of Chardonnay in Côtes de Jura and 4 ha of Savagnin in Château-Chalon. Alcoholic fermentation is followed by malolactic fermentation in cuve; then the wine is matured in barriques from Burgundy.

There are four wines: the Côtes de Jura (80% Chardonnay and 20% Savagnin), Château-Chalon, a Crémant, and Macvin. Jean Macle's reputation verged on reclusive, and with Madame Macle as the gatekeeper, it was always difficult to make appointments here, which may add to the mystique, but the domain is widely regarded as a reference point for Château-Chalon. Jean Macle's stated view was that Château-Chalon should not be drunk until 10 years after release, which is to say sixteen years after the vintage. The wine is then expected to last for a half century. All wines were produced in the traditional oxidized style until Laurent Macle introduced the first ouillé wine in 2007, showing a most elegant, refined style, albeit with only four barrels (1,000 bottles).

Domaine Louis Magnin *

90 Chemin Buis, Arbin, 73800

(33) 04 79 84 12 12

louis.magnin@wanadoo.fr

Louis Magnin

www.domainelouismagnin.fr

Arbin

Arbin Mondeuse

Chignin-Bergeron, Grand Orgue

8 ha; 30,000 bottles

Louis and Béatrice Magnin have acquired a high reputation since taking over this family domain in Savoie in 1973, when it consisted of only 4 ha. Located near Montmélian, in the valley of the Combe de Savoie, right under the massive mountain of Bauges, vineyards are on steep slopes. The domain is certified organic but follows biodynamic principles. A new cave was constructed in 2006.

The wines represent the traditions of Savoie: in the whites are Roussette de Savoie, Vin de Savoie Jacquère, and Chignin-Bergeron (100% Roussanne); there is a special cuvée, Grand Orgue, from the two oldest parcels of Roussanne. The reds are the Vin de Savoie Gamay and Arbin Mondeuse. The two major cuvées of the house are the regular Mondeuse (more than half of production), and the Roussanne (around a third). Jacquère and Roussanne are vinified in stainless steel, while the Roussette uses a small proportion of 500 liter barrels.

There are three cuvées of Arbin Mondeuse: La Rouge, vinified in steel and then matured in a large old wooden fermenter; La Brova, matured in barriques; and the Vieilles Vignes: there is also a special cuvée, Tout un Monde, from the oldest Mondeuse vines. Occasionally there are sweet wines. The domain made its reputation for its specialty of producing Mondeuse as a serious wine, although the variety is inevitably on the rustic side, especially when young, but the top cuvées become more elegant if given time.

Domaine du Pélican **

DOMAINE
DU
PÉLICAN

ARBOIS
SAVAGNIN OUILLÉ

2012

MARQUIS D'ANGERVILLE
PROPRIÉTAIRE-RÉCOLTANT A ARBOIS, JURA, FRANCE

4 *Quartier Saint Laurent, 39600 Montigny-les-Arsures*

francois.duvivier@domainedangerville.fr

Francois Duvivier

Arbois

Arbois Savagnin

15 ha

The story goes that the Marquis d'Angerville, whose estate in Volnay makes mostly red wine but has branched out into white, was dining at a restaurant in Paris where he had instructed the sommelier to bring him a Chardonnay that did not come from Burgundy. He was so impressed with the wine that he thought the sommelier had made a mistake and brought him a Burgundy, but it turned out to be from the Jura. This led to a search for vineyards in the Jura, which led to the creation of Domaine du Pélican.

The domain started by purchasing the Château de Chavanes, which had a winery and a 5 ha biodynamic vineyard. "This was important for us because we work only in biodynamics in Volnay," says François Duvivier, who came from Marquis D'Angerville to run the estate. Then we bought 5 ha in Grand Curoulet, it's one of the best places for Savagnin in Arbois, but the vineyard had been abandoned. Our most recent acquisition is from our neighbor Jacques Puffeney, who rented us his vineyards." (One of the most famous growers in Arbois, Jacques Puffeney is located a hundred yards up the street from Domaine du Pélican.)

Pélican makes only ouillé wines (in the modern, non-oxidative style). There are varietal Chardonnays and Savagnins, and a red blend of Poulsard, Trousseau and Pinot Noir, but no varietal Pinot Noir. "We don't want to produce a single Pinot Noir because it's an international variety, and me, I'm a Burgundian, so I believe Pinot Noir should come from Burgundy. We want to defend the local varieties, we will produce a varietal Trousseau in the future."

"With Chardonnay we use 228 liter barrels and 15% new oak, with Savagnin there are larger containers and no new oak barrels. The Jura is always freshness and acidity and liveliness," François says. To start with there are only single cuvées of Chardonnay and Savagnin, but in the future there will be single vineyard wines from lieu-dits Barbi and Grand Curoulet. "We've separated Barbi from the beginning, but up to now blended it, but now we understand it better and we are making a single vineyard wine." It has greater depth and minerality than the Arbois blend, but still that typical freshness of the Jura. The other lieu-dit, Grand Curoulet, has an unusual exposure. "When I arrived, I asked the geologist, are you sure, this is facing north? He was right: it is great, but if you view the terroir with Burgundian eyes, you can't understand," says François. The Savagnin has a restrained sense of salinity and minerality, with the wines from the lieu-dits again showing more concentration.

The red blend is lively and fresh, very much in the style of Jura, with a little more weight than the varietal Poulsard, which is a nice summer quaffing wine. Domaine du Pélican is a work in progress. "If you come in 2022, you can taste our first Vin Jaune. Jacques Puffeney gave us some old barrels with the lees when he racked his 2009 and we put some Savagnin from 2015 in them."

Domaine Désiré Petit

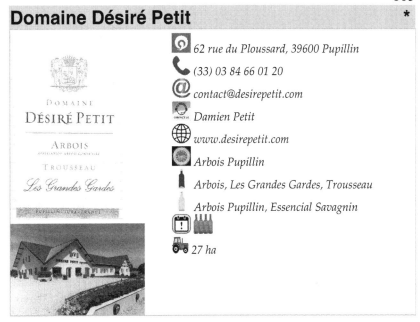

62 *rue du Ploussard, 39600 Pupillin*

(33) 03 84 66 01 20

contact@desirepetit.com

Damien Petit

www.desirepetit.com

Arbois Pupillin

Arbois, Les Grandes Gardes, Trousseau

Arbois Pupillin, Essencial Savagnin

27 *ha*

The Petit family has lived in Pupillin for centuries, and the domain was created in 1932. Désiré handed it over to his sons, Gérard and Marcel, and today it is run by Marcel's son, Damien, and his sister Anne-Laure. Most of the vineyards are in the tiny appellation of Arbois Pupillin, on steep slopes above the village. The domain is converting to organic viticulture.

The whites are mostly in the ouillé style. Both Chardonnay and Savagnin tend to an elegant mineral style; the Cuvée Tradition is a blend of 70% Chardonnay with 30% Savagnin with some oxidative influences. "I want it to have an oxidative style but not too strong," says Damien.

The reds go through carbonic maceration, but retain a fresh, elegant style, with the purity of fruits that marks the house. "I'm a fan of Gamay," Damien says, "It's important to keep the old selections," He has found a 120-year-old plot of Gamay and is propagating it by selection massale; there will be a cuvée in about five years. Most of production is sold directly from the tasting room, with little available for export.

Domaine Jacques Puffeney ★★

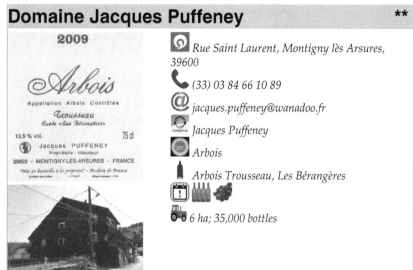

2009

Arbois

Appellation Arbois Contrôlée

Trousseau
Cuvée «Les Bérangères»

13,5 % vol.   75 cl

Jacques PUFFENEY
Propriétaire · Viticulteur

39600 · MONTIGNY-LES-ARSURES · FRANCE

Mis en bouteille à la propriété · Produit de France

Rue Saint Laurent, Montigny lès Arsures, 39600

(33) 03 84 66 10 89

jacques.puffeney@wanadoo.fr

Jacques Puffeney

Arbois

Arbois Trousseau, Les Bérangères

6 ha; 35,000 bottles

Having started as a cheese maker, and then slowly building up the domain with vineyards around the town of Arbois (starting from a tiny plot owned by his father), Jacques Puffeney is regarded as a seminal producer in the region, sometimes called "the Pope of the Jura." After fifty years of making wine, still working alone, it became necessary to reduce the size of the domain in 2012, and with no one to succeed him, in 2014 Jacques sold to Guillaume d'Angerville (of Volnay). The vineyards are now part of d'Angerville's Domaine du Pélican, which is located a hundred yards down the street. Holdings were divided between red and white, with all the traditional varieties.

Puffeney was known especially for his Trousseau, with his location in Montagny Les Arsures considered a prime site for the variety. Winemaking was traditional, with natural yeasts, extended aging in old foudres, and minimal use of sulfur. The whites had no topping up and so developed in the oxidized style, but showed a subtle hand, almost something of a half way house between the full traditional style and the modern. The Chardonnay, for example, has a mineral quality with a touch of those delicious savory notes of fenugreek. There were almost a dozen cuvées in all, including several special cuvées: Sacha, which is a blend of Chardonnay and Savagnin; Poulsard "M", which comes from vineyards in the home village; the Trousseau Les Bérangères, which comes from a tiny plot of 35-year-old vines planted by selection massale; and of course Vin Jaune. The last vintages of the domain are still on the market.

Domaine Ratte

6 rue de La Faiencerie, 39601 Arbois

(33) 06 79 28 32 94

domaine.ratte@gmail.com

Michel-Henri Ratte

www.domaine-ratte.com

Arbois

Arbois, Trousseau À La Dame

Arbois, Melon d'Arbois

8 ha

Formerly a grower, Michel-Henri Ratte left the cooperative in 2014 and started to produce his own wine with the 2015 vintage. This small family concern is run by Michel-Henri together with his wife François and son Quentin. They have started with two whites and three reds, all in the Arbois appellation. There is one Chardonnay and one Savagnin, both in ouillé style—"we only have ouillé style," François explains, "because we have only just started and haven't had long enough yet to mature wines under voile."

The three reds are a Pinot Noir, a Trousseau À La Dame (the name refers to the cultivar, which is a rare variant with small clusters),—and the Rubis cuvée, which is an unusual field blend of old vines of Trousseau, Poulsard, and Pinot Noir (planted as a mixed plot by François's grandfather more than eighty years ago). The whites are elegant and pure, the reds tend to be spicy, with Trousseau À La Dame showing the greatest depth, and unusual refinement for the variety. The domain has made a most promising start.

Domaine Rolet Père Et Fils   *

11 Rue Hotel de Ville, Arbois, 39600

(33) 03 84 66 00 05

info@rolet-arbois.com

Pierre Rolet

www.rolet-arbois.com

Arbois

Côtes de Jura, La Dent de Charnet, Chardonnay

Arbois, Tradition

62 ha; 350,000 bottles

The estate was created in 1942 by Désiré Rolet, and today is run by four siblings of the second generation, Bernard (viticulturalist), Guy (wine-maker), Pierre and Éliane (marketing). This is the second largest, and most extended, domain in the Jura, with vineyard holdings in many areas. It's a go-ahead operation with a tasting room in the center of the town of Arbois that offers almost all the wines.

The modern facility includes stainless steel cuves and barriques, including some new wood, which are used depending on the cuvée. About half the vines are more than fifty years old; the others are regarded as young vines. Plantings are divided roughly equally between white and black varieties. There are vineyards in Arbois (at 36 ha comprising just over half), the Côtes de Jura (21 ha), and most recently an addition of 3 ha in l' Étoile.

There is a correspondingly large range of wines. The nine white wine cuvées comprise four Arbois, four Côtes du Jura, and an Étoile; they include Savagnin, and blends of Savagnin with Chardonnay, in both ouillé and oxidized styles. The Tradition cuvée is a blend of Chardonnay matured in ouillé style with Savagnin matured under voile, and is the most subtle of the blended cuvées, but all have quite intense Sherry-like character. The Côtes de Jura Savagnin offers a fine example of the style of Vin Jaune without the weight. The Étoile is pure Chardonnay. I like the Côtes de Jura Chardonnay for the light savory edge, whereas the Harmonie cuvée from Arbois is heavier, reflecting its aging in new oak barriques.

The reds mostly come from Arbois, including separate monovarietal cuvées for Pinot Noir, Poulsard, and Trousseau, as well as Les Grandvaux (an equal blend of Pinot Noir and Poulsard), and a classic assemblage of all three. There are also several Crémants, as well as Vin Jaune and Vin de Paille from Arbois (and of course Macvin).

The style is relatively forceful, with spicy, nutty impressions for the ouillé Chardonnays, quite a strong oxidative influence for the Tradition cuvée, strong savory impressions for the Savagnin under voile, and a savory but subtle Vin Jaune. The wines are regarded as being among the most reliable of the Jura.

Domaine André et Mireille Tissot ★★

39600 Montigny lès Arsures

(33) 03 84 66 08 27

stephane.tissot.arbois@wanadoo.fr

Stéphane Tissot

www.stephane-tissot.com

Arbois

Arbois Pinot Noir, Sous La Tour

Arbois Vin Jaune, La Vasée

Arbois Chardonnay, Les Bruyères

50 ha; 140,000 bottles

One of the most interesting producers in the Jura, Stéphane Tissot has built a great reputation since he took over the family domain a few years ago. His name has been prominent on the label for quite a while, but the name of the domain has now changed on the label to Bénédict & Stéphane Tissot. The domain started with 10 ha in 1950 with Stéphane's grandfather, who was a vigneron. The focus is on terroir. "Land is not expensive, although vines of quality cost more," Stéphane says. There are 42 ha in Arbois, 2 ha in Château-Chalon, and 6 ha on Côtes de Jura. Vineyards are a mix of large holdings and some very small parcels. All the vineyards are maintained by selection massale. Most of the wines come from the Arbois appellation.

Plantings are split equally between black and white grapes, but there is less red wine production because many of the black grapes, from the less interesting terroirs, go into Crémant, which is a quarter of production. The Indigène Crémant comes from the same base wine as the Brut Nature, but is fermented with indigenous instead of cultured yeast, giving a more flavorful impression.

Most of the white wine production is Chardonnay, which is vinified by parcel to give seven different cuvées. The house style offers a smoky, spicy introduction, following to a palate varying from mineral to more opulent, depending on the terroir, with a finish that tends to a savory impression in the direction of tarragon. La Mailloche is the richest—"This is always a little more rustic," says Stéphane. Les Bruyères shows the domain's characteristic smokiness and spiciness—"This is completely different, with a very strong Jurassien expression," is how Stéphane describes it. And Le Clos de la Tour de Curon comes from vines replanted in 2002 at 12,000 plants per hectare, and achieves very low yields. With two year's élevage, this is always the most concentrated (and most alcoholic) of Tissot's whites. All the wines have a distinctive savory orientation.

The Arbois Savagnin, which spends 26 months under voile, is very savory, and more subtle than the Vin Jaune. La Vasée is the most mineral and savory of the three Vin Jaune cuvées, which are all very fine. "We look for finesse and elegance, there are many people who look for power," Stéphane says.

The reds are light and fresh, and at their best can show an earthy character. Pinot Noir is the most interesting, and the cuvée Sous La Tour is a fine example of the authentic style of Arbois, mineral and earthy, with some aging potential.

It's very lively at the domain, there are lots of experiments. One of Stéphane's most common words is experimentation, and if there's one word to describe Tissot, it's originality. Going round the vineyards or tasting with Stéphane is a whirlwind of activity. There is now a tasting room in the town of Arbois where some of the 36 cuvées of the domain can be tried.

Index of Estates by Rating

3 star

Château de Beauregard

Domaine Vincent Dureuil-Janthial

Château des Jacques

Maison Verget

2 star

Domaine Jules Desjourneys

Domaine Ferret

Château-Fuissé

Domaine Paul Janin et Fils

Domaine Marcel Lapierre

Domaine du Pélican

Domaine Jacques Puffeney

Domaine Saumaize-Michelin

Julien Sunier

Domaine André et Mireille Tissot

1 star

Domaine Stéphane Aladame

Domaine Daniel et Martine Barraud

Domaine David-Beaupère

Domaine Berthet-Bondet

Domaine André Bonhomme

Domaine Jean Bourdy

Château de Chamirey

Domaine du Clos du Fief

Domaine Louis et Claude Desvignes

Georges Duboeuf

Domaine Daniel Dugois

Domaine Jean Foillard

Domaine Ganevat

Domaine Mee Godard

Domaine de la Grand'Cour

Domaine des Vignes du Maynes

Maison Paul et Marie Jacqueson

Domaine Joblot

Domaine Michel Juillot

Domaine Héritiers du Comte Lafon

Domaine Jean-Claude Lapalu

Domaine Bruno Lorenzon

Domaine François Lumpp

Domaine Macle

Domaine Louis Magnin

Domaine Désiré Petit

Dominique Piron

Domaine François Raquillet

Domaine Ratte

Domaine Coudert Clos de La Roilette

Domaine Rolet Père Et Fils

Domaine des Souchons

Domaine La Soufrandière

Domaine des Terres Dorées

Domaine Jean Thévenet

Domaine Thibert Père et Fils

Domaine Aubert et Pamela De Villaine

Index of Organic and Biodynamic Estates

Index of Estates by Appellation

Domaine Héritiers du Comte Lafon
Maison Verget

Mercurey

Château de Chamirey
Domaine Michel Juillot
Domaine Bruno Lorenzon
Domaine François Raquillet

Montagny

Domaine Stéphane Aladame

Morgon

Domaine Louis et Claude Desvignes
Domaine Jean Foillard
Domaine Mee Godard
Domaine Marcel Lapierre
Dominique Piron
Domaine des Souchons
Julien Sunier

Moulin-à-Vent

Domaine Jules Desjourneys
Château des Jacques
Domaine Paul Janin et Fils

Pouilly-Fuissé

Domaine Daniel et Martine Barraud
Château de Beauregard
Domaine Ferret
Château-Fuissé
Domaine Saumaize-Michelin
Domaine Thibert Père et Fils

Pouilly-Vinzelles

Domaine La Soufrandière

Rully

Domaine Vincent Dureuil-Janthial
Maison Paul et Marie Jacqueson

Viré-Clessé

Domaine André Bonhomme
Domaine Jean Thévenet

Index of Estates by Name

BOOKS by Benjamin Lewin MW

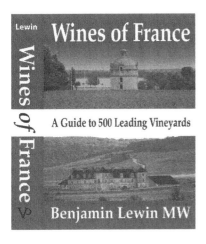

Wines of France

This comprehensive account of the vineyards and wines of France today is extensively illustrated with photographs and maps of each wine-producing area. Leading vineyards and winemakers are profiled in detail, with suggestions for wines to try and vineyards to visit.

In Search of Pinot Noir

Pinot Noir is a uniquely challenging grape with an unrivalled ability to reflect the character of the site where it grows. This world wide survey of everywhere Pinot Noir is grown extends from Burgundy to the New World, and profiles leading producers.

23998904R00072

Printed in Poland
by Amazon Fulfillment
Poland Sp. z o.o., Wrocław